THE LAWS OF ARMS IN ENGLAND, FRANCE & SCOTLAND

BY

IAN DE MINVIELLE-DEVAUX

First Edition
(Reissued)

The Laws of Arms in England, France & Scotland
By Ian de Minvielle-Devaux

ISBN Hard Cover edition: 978-1-4196-7424-2
ISBN Soft Cover edition: 978-1-4196-7425-9

Cover Image: *Map of Europe about 1560*, from *The Historical Atlas* by William R. Shepherd, 1923.

BookSurge Publishing
www.booksurge.com
1-866-308-6235
orders@booksurge.com

CONTENTS

PREFACE TO THIS
REISSUED FIRST EDITION

This is a republication, in a different format, of a text which was originally published in a limited edition in 1988. The intention is to make the text available to anyone whose interest in heraldry in England, France or Scotland extends beyond the art of composing coats of arms.

No attempt has been made to bring in any changes which may have occurred since 1988, such as the rulings about the bearing of arms by women made by the English Kings of Arms in 1995 and 1997, or the change in the way in which a new Lord Lyon is selected following the establishment of the Scottish Parliament. However, the opportunity has been taken to correct minor errors of fact in the account of the French heralds and in the timing of some of the fees involved in registering arms in the French Armorial Général created in 1696.

A more detailed study of the French laws of arms is in preparation. It will incorporate material from the present text together with much additional information.

I am grateful to Mr Adrian A. Barham who has made this republication possible. Mr Barham is himself engaged in a review of the legal aspects of English heraldry, and I hope that the fruits of his studies will soon be made available to the public.

I.M.D.
September 2007

PREFACE TO THE FIRST EDITION

The use of arms was initially governed by custom, but eventually there came to be developed, in each of England, France and Scotland, a body of laws within the jurisdiction of courts of law.

Our primary purpose is to try to ascertain the principal aspects of the laws of arms in each of these countries, and to demonstrate some of the similarities and some of the differences between the three systems.

The most authoritative sources of the laws of arms are, firstly, enactments of the Sovereign in accordance with the constitution of each country, and secondly, judgments of the courts having jurisdiction in this branch of law. Failing these, we must have regard to the rules and practices of the principal executive officers, acting within the scope of the powers delegated to them by the Sovereigns. We have, wherever possible, relied on such authorities.

In some matters there are no direct authorities, and there guidance may be sought from long established practice or even from the opinions of commentators, but the rules which may be deduced from such sources should not be considered to be settled law. This should be borne in mind when the following pages are being read.

Some brief attention will be given to historical development, but only insofar as this may help us to ascertain the laws of arms in their most evolved state, which in England and Scotland means the laws as they exist now, but in France means the laws as they existed before arms were abolished by the French Revolution. (Nowadays, the use of arms is no longer illegal in France, but the only rule of law relating thereto is that no family may use arms associated with another existing family; it is up to a user of arms to choose to follow any, or none, of the other rules which formerly applied.)

We have tried to approach our subject with an open mind, wishing only to find out what the laws of arms are, and not concerned with what they should be. If we have misunderstood or misinterpreted some point, we would be very happy to be corrected.

Our study is confined to the laws affecting the arms of private persons; we shall therefore ignore arms of sovereignty, arms of public bodies, arms of office and ecclesiastical arms. Flags and badges are outside our field.

We shall say little about the nature and the arrangement of the charges borne on shields. Most of the "rules" relating thereto are conventions without legal force. These rules, which are mostly very similar in the three countries, are described in innumerable textbooks of heraldry.

Most of the material on which this work is based is derived from the publications of a multitude of earlier authors who are listed in the General Bibliography, but particular tribute should be paid to Sir Anthony Wagner and Mr G. D. Squibb in England, to Monsieur Rémi Mathieu in France, and to Sir Thomas Innes of Learney in Scotland.

More particular identification of the sources of many of the paragraphs of the present work will be found in the numbered Notes to each Chapter. Some of the Notes contain supplementary information or discussion.

I.M.D.

CHAPTER 1

INTRODUCTION

The use of arms, as fixed hereditary marks of identification displayed on shields, banners, garments and seals, may have begun in the lands between the Loire and the Rhine. In the twelfth and thirteenth centuries it spread through Western Europe and beyond, soon becoming generalised among the upper ranks of society.

The ceaseless flow of wars, battles, chevauchées, crusades, tournaments, threw the nobles and soldiers of Western Europe together at various times and places, and this both facilitated and made necessary the observance of common rules as to the form and display of arms.

The constant intercourse between England, France and Scotland, caused in part by the French wars and the Scottish wars, the possession of large parts of France by the King of England, the sojourns, often willing, of Scottish nobles in France, or often unwilling, of French and Scottish nobles in England, favoured a particularly uniform development of customs and laws in those countries. These unifying factors lessened in and especially after the fifteenth century, and thereafter each country developed more special laws and customs of its own.

As certain customs hardened with time, they came to be looked upon as laws. At the same time the Kings of these increasingly centralised monarchies found it natural and indeed necessary to extend their control over a matter which was so closely associated with war, with a display of lordship or power, and with social status. The precise import of an order of King Henry V of England in 1417 may be a matter of some dispute, but it demonstrates that by that date a Sovereign might think it worthwhile to lay down rules as to the lawful use of arms. An Act of the Scottish Parliament of 1430 indicates that every freeholder was expected to have a seal of his arms. In the statutes of the

Order of St. Michael promulgated by King Louis XI of France in 1469, it was specified that every knight of the order must be a gentleman of name and arms.(1)

Even before these dates, Kings or their representatives had been making grants of arms and judging disputes about the ownership of arms. Some examples will be mentioned in later chapters.

The exercise of royal control over arms involved three essential functions of sovereignty: the legislative function, the judicial function and the executive function.

The legislative function has been exercised by the laying down of laws. The judicial function, originally exercised by the King himself (as in Richard II's judgment of the appeal in the case of Scrope v. Grosvenor), came to be exercised on his behalf by judges; this function, which involves interpreting legislation and declaring the law on aspects which have not been the subject of legislation, is of great importance in elucidating the law. The executive function has been exercised especially in the granting of arms, either by the King himself or by his deputies appointed for the purpose - the Kings of Arms.

CHAPTER 2

LEGISLATION

In each country the sovereign authority may create new laws by legislation in accordance with the particular constitution of that country.

In England the highest source of legislation in post-medieval times has been the King (or Queen) acting with the consent of Parliament to produce an enactment known as an Act of Parliament. There have in fact been no Acts of Parliament relating to the bearing of arms in England (apart from some purely fiscal measures). On a lower level than an Act of Parliament (in that an Act can limit or supersede it) is the exercise of the Royal Prerogative, for example by an Order in Council or a Proclamation. An instance is an Order in Council of Charles II in 1674, confirming a Declaration of 1673, defining the powers of the Earl Marshal of England; this still has effect today. Certain other exercises of the Royal Prerogative may be considered to be quasi-legislative acts; examples are the various Commissions of Visitation between 1530 and 1687 defining the powers of the commissioners; Letters Patent of James I in 1622, of Charles II in 1672 and of James II in 1687 in favour of the Earl Marshal and relating to the holding of the Court of Chivalry; and Letters Patent of the Kings and Queens creating new Kings of Arms and specifying some of their powers.(1)

In France the King alone was the source of all higher legislation. In post-medieval times he made new laws by means of Edicts and Ordinances, and modified or added detail to them by means of Declarations or Orders in Council ("Arrêts du Conseil"). Certain Edicts or Ordinances of 1560, 1579, 1583 and 1634 contained provisions about the use of timbred arms as did Declarations of 1656, 1661 and 1665, and a particular Declaration of 1699 relating to the province of Franche-Comté. An Ordinance of 1556 forbade changes of arms in Normandy, but was repealed soon after its promulgation. An Edict of 1615 created the post of

Juge d'Armes; abolished by an Edict of 1696, it was restored by an Edict of 1701. The powers of the Juge d'Armes were further defined by an Order in Council of 1706. An Ordinance of 1629 contained a provision as to the differencing of the arms of bastards; it was supplemented by a Declaration of 1697. A Declaration of 1699 confirmed a prohibition on the bearing of undifferenced arms by cadets in certain provinces. An Edict of 1696 created an Armorial Général; it was supplemented by another Edict of 1700 and by a number of Orders in Council.(2)

It became an accepted constitutional rule that new laws did not come into force until they had been registered by the courts which were to enforce them, especially the "sovereign" courts (Parlements etc.) which will be mentioned in Chapter 3. This eventually gave these bodies a degree of political influence; they could delay or even refuse registration of a new law, although, if the King insisted, there were procedures by which he could force them to register the new law. This rule was invoked to prevent the coming into force of an Ordinance of 1760 on the registration of arms.

In Scotland there have been several Acts of Parliament relating to the bearing of arms, of which the most important have been Acts of the Scottish Parliament of 1592 and 1672, and an Act of the British Parliament of 1867. These Acts, and especially that of 1672, have had a profound effect, as will be seen hereafter. Letters Patent creating new Lords Lyon Kings of Arms and specifying some of their powers were originally exercises of the unfettered Royal Prerogative, but in this matter the Royal Prerogative is at once subject to and supported by the provisions of the above Acts of Parliament.(3)

CHAPTER 3

THE JUDICIARY

Armorial causes were within the jurisdiction of the usual royal courts of France, whereas in England and in Scotland they have normally been heard by special courts.

In England it is the Court of Chivalry which has exclusive jurisdiction in armorial matters. It seems to have come into existence in the fourteenth century, mainly for the purpose of judging certain matters arising from war, and the judges were the Constable of England, who was commander in chief of the troops in the King's absence, and the Marshal of England, who had ancillary functions. Since the early sixteenth century the office of Constable has been left unfilled (except for certain brief periods), but the Court has continued to hear causes relating to arms under the Earl Marshal of England as sole judge, although there have been long periods (for example in the seventeenth century and between 1737 and 1954) when the Court has been dormant. The law applied by the Court of Chivalry is the English Law of Arms, or what a witness in 1408 called "the law of arms as used in England", and is consequently not necessarily the same as the law of arms in other countries. The procedures of the Court are those of the Civil (Roman-based) Law rather than those of the English Common Law.(1)

The jurisdiction of the Court of Chivalry under the Earl Marshal as sole judge was stated and confirmed by Letters Patent of James I in 1622, of Charles II in 1672, and of James II in 1687, and was affirmed in a judgment of the Lord Chief Justice of England, acting as the Earl Marshal's surrogate, in a case heard in the Court of Chivalry in 1954.

A Declaration of Charles II in 1673, confirmed by an Order in Council in 1674, defined the powers of the Earl Marshal as including the judging of "all matters touching arms, ensigns of nobility, honour and chivalry according to the law of arms".

By Letters Patent of 1672 Charles II vested the office of "Earl Marshal of England" in Henry Lord Howard and in the heirs male of his body. He became Duke of Norfolk in 1677, and the office thus became hereditary in the holders of that Dukedom. As each Duke succeeds to the title, he is personally invested by the Sovereign who hands him the baton which is symbolic of his office as Earl Marshal.

The Earl Marshal is not usually a lawyer, and it has long been customary for him to appoint a lawyer as his surrogate or lieutenant to perform his judicial duties. This practice is to be distinguished from the appointment by the Crown of Commissioners to perform the duties of Earl Marshal at times when there has been no Earl Marshal, and from the appointment by the Earl Marshal himself, with the Crown's approval, of a Deputy Earl Marshal at times when the Earl Marshal has been unable to act, for example for religious reasons. Such Commissioners and Deputies could perform all the functions of the Earl Marshal, whereas a surrogate or lieutenant only acts for him in his judicial capacity.

An officer of the Court of Chivalry appointed by the Crown and called the Queen's (or King's) Advocate could act as "public prosecutor" in causes of office brought against persons who broke the laws of arms. No Queen's Advocate has been appointed since the eighteenth century, but it seems that his duties may have devolved on the Attorney General. Causes of office can also be promoted by others, for example the Kings of Arms, who are not officers of the Court of Chivalry. Causes *inter partes*, that is, disputes between persons or companies, are called causes of instance.

The records of the Court of Chivalry are in the keeping of the Register who, with various inferior officers, is appointed by the Earl Marshal.

The jurisdiction of the Court of Chivalry in heraldic matters is derived from custom. Such matters were in issue in the earliest known cases in that Court. Acts of Parliament of 1384, 1389 and 1399 had the effect of preserving the Court's jurisdiction in heraldic matters, and the repeal of these statutes by an Act of Parliament of 1881 did not alter this. The exclusive jurisdiction of the Court of Chivalry in heraldic matters was affirmed in the judgment in the case heard in 1954 which has already been mentioned.

In this case, the only one since 1737, a company which had usurped the arms granted to a city was enjoined to cease this usurpation. As this case illustrates, the Earl Marshal can judge the lawfulness of arms and can protect rights in arms.

The English Kings of Arms and other heralds are not officers of the Court of Chivalry, although they may appear in the role of expert witnesses, and the Court has sometimes referred a point to them for a report thereon. In general, their functions are essentially executive, but some of them involve quasi-judicial aspects, as when they assess the right of a person to particular arms. More clearly judicial were the powers granted to particular heralds under a Visitation Commission.

The heralds on Visitation have been likened to Common Law judges on circuit. Persons failing to obey a summons to appear before the Visitation Heralds, or refusing to conform to their decisions, could be ordered to appear before the Earl Marshal to justify themselves. As there have been no Visitations since the Revolution of 1688, these powers have not existed for three centuries.

Appeals from the Court of Chivalry could be taken in medieval times to the Crown itself. Thus it was Richard II who pronounced the final judgment in 1390 in the case of Scrope v. Grosvenor. In the seventeenth century such appeals were taken to a special Court of Delegates. Changes in appeal procedures in the nineteenth century had the effect that appeals from the Court of Chivalry would have lain to the Judicial Committee of the Privy Council. However, an Act of Parliament of 1963 appears to have had the effect of abolishing this provision, and it seems that there is at present no effective possibility of appealing from a judgment of the Court of Chivalry.(2)

The Court of Chivalry, being an inferior court, is subject to an order of prohibition from the High Court which would lie, for example, if the former court attempted to exceed its jurisdiction.(3)

If a person desirous of initiating litigation in the Court of Chivalry were to be refused permission to do so, it seems that he could apply to the High Court for an order of mandamus to oblige the Court of Chivalry to sit and hear his case.(4)

The remedies which are available to the Court of Chivalry include imposing fines, awarding damages or costs, and "monishing" or ordering a party to do or abstain from doing something. At one time this court could commit for contempt. At the present time a party refusing to obey the Court could be declared in contempt of court and could be committed to gaol by the High Court.

Scotland too has a special court for armorial causes, but this court has nothing to do with either Constable or Marshal. There was (and indeed still is) a Constable of Scotland who, as in England, was a military commander and judge of military affairs. There was also, until the eighteenth century, an Earl Marshal or Earl Marischal of Scotland. Until at least the seventeenth century there was a Court of the Marischal which in 1633 judged a case relating to riotous behaviour which threatened to lead to fighting. Nisbet appears to have thought that the Earl Marischal's Court had power to judge differences relating to arms, but this seems not to have been the case if by "arms" is meant heraldic ensigns rather than weapons.(5)

The Scottish court for armorial causes is the Court of the Lord Lyon, or Lyon Court, which has been functioning since at least the early sixteenth century. The judge of this court is the Lord Lyon King of Arms. The Lord Lyon is appointed by Letters Patent of the Sovereign under the Great Seal (or, since the eighteenth century, under the seal appointed to be used in

Scotland in place of the Great Seal). His appointment, like that of other Scottish judges, is nowadays made on the advice of the Secretary of State for Scotland.(6)

In the seventeenth and eighteenth centuries the Lord Lyon's duties were often performed by a Lyon Depute. Most Lyons Depute were qualified lawyers (Advocates or Writers to the Signet). After the middle of the eighteenth century all Lyons Depute were qualified lawyers. Since 1866 there have been no Lyons Depute and all Lords Lyon have been qualified lawyers, except during a brief period in 1927-1929.

The records of Lyon Court are in the keeping of the Lyon Clerk, who is also appointed by the Crown.

There is a Procurator Fiscal (appointed by the Lord Lyon) who acts as "public prosecutor" against, for example, persons (especially but not exclusively traders) displaying illegal arms.

The Scottish heralds other than the Lord Lyon are not officers of the Court.

The procedures in Lyon Court appear to conform generally to those of the old Scottish courts. Lyon Court exercises both a civil and a penal jurisdiction under the old common law of Scotland, and under Acts of the Scottish Parliament of 1592 and 1672 and a confirmatory Act of Parliament of 1867. The Lord Lyon judges rights to arms. He protects arms; for example a recorded holder of arms can obtain a judicial injunction ("interdict") to restrain others from using his arms. The Procurator Fiscal can bring proceedings against users of unlawful arms, such as any arms which have not been recorded ("matriculated") in the Lord Lyon's registers as required by the Act of 1672.

In the eighteenth century there were many cases against users of illegal arms, including a number of peers and lairds. Such actions still continue, although the receipt of the Lord Lyon's writ ("precept") initiating legal action, or even a mere warning, is often enough to cause those concerned to desist from their illegal acts.

A substantial amount of business in Lyon Court flows from the provision in the 1672 Act which restricts the lawful bearing of arms to those persons whose arms have been matriculated in the Lord Lyon's registers, as well as the requirement for all arms to be duly differenced. Strictly speaking, it seems that every transmission of Scottish arms should give rise to matriculation proceedings. However, it seems to be customary to allow some generations to elapse between successive matriculations of particular arms by the heirs to those arms, especially where the succession is a straightforward one. Any variation from such a straightforward succession requires matriculation; for example an alteration in the destination of the arms, or the taking up of the name and arms by the son of an heiress who has previously used his father's name, or the addition of a quarter to the arms for any reason, must be the subject of a matriculation, which will be allowed only when the Lord Lyon is satisfied that it is justified. The allowance of a permanently differenced version of the arms to a cadet (which in effect creates new arms) necessitates either fresh Letters Patent or, as is usual nowadays, a matriculation. Whereas a grant of arms by Letters Patent is a ministerial act, matriculation proceedings generally involve the Lord Lyon acting in his judicial capacity to determine, on the evidence before him, a right either to the whole arms or to a differenced version thereof (or to no arms at all); or to determine the most correct or efficacious manner, according to the Scottish law of arms, of dealing with some point placed before him. In the case of a right to arms, the Lord Lyon's judgment ("interlocutor") may grant warrant to the Lyon Clerk to matriculate arms, in the precise form ordered by the Lord Lyon, in the name of the person in whose favour the interlocutor issues.(7)

Between 1630 and the Treaty of Union of England and Scotland in 1707 there was a possibility of appealing from an interlocutor of Lyon Court to the Scottish Privy Council. In recent times appeals have been entertained in some matters by the Court of Session, with a possible further appeal to the House of Lords, but there may be matters, especially those of a purely armorial nature, in which appeals do not lie. In certain circumstances it is possible to apply to the Court of Session for a reduction of a Lyon Court decree on the ground that it contravenes the Acts of 1592 and 1672; this would be not an appeal but an action to ensure that a statutory right was not denied.(8)

Among the powers of Lyon Court is that of imposing a fine up to £100. More significant nowadays is its power to order the forfeiture, for the benefit of the Crown, of articles or goods bearing unlawful arms. Judicial injunctions ("interdicts") are also granted by the Court, as mentioned above. Warrants for imprisonment were issued by the Lord Lyon himself as recently as the eighteenth century.

As has been indicated, most of the English and Scottish litigation involving armorial matters has taken place in the special courts we have discussed, rather than in the ordinary royal courts. In England the ordinary courts are considered to have no juris-diction in matters relating to dignities, and as the right to bear arms is (according to judicial statements) a dignity, these courts have generally confined themselves to matters which are not armorial, even if some of the cases they have heard have also involved arms in such a way that some regard has had to be paid to the arms, as where a court is giving effect to a disposition of property conditional on the taking up of certain arms. The Scottish Court of Session seems to have been more willing than the corresponding English courts to deal with matters related to arms. One reason may be that in Scotland arms are considered to be heritable property as well as a dignity.(9)

The situation was different in France, where the great majority of cases involving arms were litigated in the ordinary royal courts, although there were also some special tribunals with some jurisdiction in such matters.

The ordinary royal courts of France exercised jurisdiction in armorial matters as early as the fifteenth century. Two levels of these courts were mainly used, the lower being that of the

11

Bailiwicks ("Bailliages") and Seneschalcies ("Sénéchaussées") and the upper being that of the Parlements and similar bodies.

The Bailiwicks and Seneschalcies (which were numerous) were the lowest royal courts which could hear cases involving the nobles, and this gave them jurisdiction in various nobiliary and armorial matters, including testamentary conditions of name and arms, and the right to the undifferenced arms of a family. (10)

The Parlements were "sovereign" courts in that there could be no appeal from their judgments (although the King always retained the power to issue an Order ("Arrêt") of his Council quashing such a judgment). The Parlements, like the Bailiwicks and Seneschalcies, had a territorial distribution, but the area covered by each Parlement was usually much greater than that covered by each of these inferior courts. The Parlement of Paris exercised its jurisdiction over nearly a third of the kingdom. Some of the large provinces had their own Parlements. A few areas added to the kingdom at a relatively late date had small Parlements known as Conseils Souverains or Conseils Supérieurs, as had the colonies.(11)

The Parlements and Conseils Souverains had a very wide jurisdiction which was exercised in some cases on appeal from the Bailiwicks and Seneschalcies and in other cases in actions originating in these courts themselves. Among the causes of a heraldic nature which were decided by these courts were a number relating to the usurpation of the arms of another family, the right to the undifferenced arms of one's own family, name and arms clauses in wills, and "relèvements d'armoiries", that is, the taking up (usually by a relation) of the arms of an extinct family. (12)

Other courts to be mentioned are the Cours des Aides, of which there was one in Paris and others in some of the provinces. These courts judged cases arising from the collection of certain taxes which might come to them directly or on appeal from certain lower tax tribunals. The Cours des Aides, like the Parlements, were "sovereign" courts in that there was no appeal from their judgments. As the nobles were exempt from certain taxes in certain parts of France, the Cours des Aides had some jurisdiction in questions of nobility, and this in turn gave them competence in some heraldic matters, in that they could hear cases against persons accused of usurping nobility and timbred arms. Some hundreds of such cases were judged by the Cour des Aides of Paris in the seventeenth century.(13)

The King in Council retained a supervisory power over all his courts. He could (as we have seen) quash a judgment of a "sovereign" court. The Royal Council sometimes acted more directly. Thus it could deprive someone (generally a military officer guilty of cowardice or a subject guilty of the crime of "lèse-majesté") of the ability to bear arms. Further duties of a judicial nature came to the Royal Council as a result of the Edict of 1696 creating the Armorial Général which is described in Chapter 9; it was originally intended that disputes relating to the application of this Edict should be judged by special tribunals to be known as "Maîtrises", but these were never set up and such disputes were in fact decided by the local Intendant or, on appeal, by the Royal Council.(14)

In 1615 an Edict of Louis XIII created the office of Juge d'Armes. In spite of the name, this office turned out to be mainly executive, but it did have certain judicial attributes. The Edict stated that the Juge d'Armes would have power to judge infringements of heraldic rules and to judge disputes between individuals about heraldic matters. It was contemplated that the existing French heralds might be called upon to act as advisers or assessors to assist the Juge d'Armes, but they failed to take advantage of the opportunity to play a part in the judicial process. In the event, the exercise of judicial power by the Juge d'Armes was limited. Although it seems that the original intention was to give the Juge d'Armes an exclusive jurisdiction in heraldic matters, he was never given the necessary court facilities or personnel. A few disputes were submitted to him from time to time, but most litigation relating to heraldic matters continued to be judged by the usual royal courts.(15)

13

There existed in medieval France a Court of the Constable and Marshals which was in some respects analogous to the English Court of Chivalry, which at that time was called the Court of the Constable and Marshal. The primary function of both these courts was to decide cases touching military matters. The office of Constable of France ceased to exist in the first half of the seventeenth century, but the French Court continued to exist under the Marshals of France. In later times it was particularly concerned with affairs of honour between members of the nobility. Its jurisdiction (if any) in heraldic matters before 1615 is uncertain, but after that date the Marshals' Court ("Tribunal des Maréchaux de France") could hear appeals from the Juge d'Armes.(16)

Applied (as they usually were) by the ordinary royal courts of law following their own ordinary procedures, the laws of arms of France formed part of the ordinary civil and criminal laws administered by these courts. The remedies applied and enforced by the courts in armorial causes were those generally available to them, and included for example fines and orders (injunctions).

In order to be able to judge the transmission of arms by inheritance, for example the devolution of the undifferenced chief arms of a family, it is practically necessary for the court concerned to judge the relevant pedigree. Accordingly it has long been accepted that courts having jurisdiction over arms have jurisdiction over pedigrees. Indeed it has been said, with reference at least to England and Scotland, that matters of pedigree belong to the laws of arms. The jurisdiction both of the English Court of Chivalry and of the Scottish Lyon Court has been exercised and affirmed by those courts themselves. In France the broad jurisdiction of the Parlements included the judging of pedigrees. Other bodies such as the Juge d'Armes were sometimes entrusted by the Crown with the duty of judging certain pedigrees. It might be said the English heralds on Visitation were inherently provided with a similar power which was necessary to enable them to discharge their Visitation duties.(17)

We have seen that one Scottish herald, the Lord Lyon, is also a judge, and that certain English heralds, though not judges, have exercised a degree of judicial power, for example in relation to the Visitations. The French heralds, even before their almost complete eclipse in the seventeenth century (which will be described in the next Chapter), seem never to have had any judicial power at all. Some commentators suggested that armorial disputes should be settled by the heralds, but they had no means of enforcing their decisions. If a dispute was submitted to them (as happened in 1531 when the parties to an armorial dispute put the matter before three French Kings of Arms) the decision was a private thing, and was not enforceable unless confirmed by a court.(18)

CHAPTER 4

THE OFFICERS OF ARMS

There were persons called "heralds" in France and in Britain in the thirteenth century. They were prominent in the organising and running of tournaments, and this function made it necessary for them to familiarise themselves with the arms of the nobles who took part in tournaments and with the proper ways of displaying these arms. This led to the heralds being looked upon as experts in armorial matters. This eventually became their principal function.(1)

The most astute and knowledgeable heralds attracted the favour of kings or great nobles who took them into their households, and who thereafter had the control of their duties and of their discipline. The principal heralds were invested with the title of King of Arms. In addition to these Kings of Arms and to the "ordinary" heralds, there were junior or "trainee" heralds known as pursuivants. It was customary for each heraldic post to have a name, territorial or otherwise, and for heralds holding such posts to be known by the name of the post.

In the fourteenth and early fifteenth centuries there were (as far as is known) no great differences in the ranks, powers and duties of the heraldic establishments in France, England and Scotland. Later these matters evolved differently as between the three countries. We shall see that the powers of the French heralds dwindled so that by the seventeenth century their status was low, and the most they could do was to advise those who chose to consult them. The French King felt it necessary to create a new office, that of "Juge d'Armes", to perform more substantial armorial functions. In England the powers of the heralds grew rather than diminished, while in Scotland the chief herald, or King of Arms, had his powers reinforced by statute so that they became more extensive than those exercised by any herald in France or even in England.

A herald named Mountjoy ("Montjoie") was the chief herald or King of Arms of France in much of the fifteenth century. The title of King of Arms of the French which was sometimes given to him suggests that he had, or claimed to have, an overall jurisdiction over all Frenchmen. There was an analogous implication in the title of the principal herald of England, Garter (Principal) King of Arms of Englishmen. In a petition to King Henry V, the first Garter based a request (that he be given certain garments worn by peers at their creation) on the fact that this was a prerogative of Mountjoy; this suggests that there was a tendancy for Garter to model himself on Mountjoy.(2)

In early times there were other French heralds besides Mountjoy who had titles of Kings of Arms. At least some of them appear to have derived the title from the fact that they or their predecessors were the principal heralds in some of the more or less independent dukedoms and counties (Anjou, Brittany, Burgundy, Dauphiny,...) which became provinces of the Kingdom of France at about the end of the medieval period. Several heralds with such provincial names but (after the earlier period) without the title of King of Arms continued to exist until the end of the Ancien Régime. They seem to have been in some way subordinate to, or at least of lower status than Mountjoy.(3)

By the seventeenth century there was only one French herald with the title of King of Arms, sometimes known as "Mountjoy", as well as a variable number of ordinary heralds and a few pursuivants. (There was also a herald attached to the Order of the Holy Ghost who was often called the King of Arms of the Order.) By the end of that century none of these officers seems to have had any real armorial function, although they continued to perform certain ceremonial duties.(4)

The King of England had several Kings of Arms in the fifteenth century, including one, Guyenne or Aquitaine, who was named after his possessions in France. Apart from Ireland King of Arms (precursor of Ulster King of Arms), the only ones to survive the fifteenth century were Clarenceux and Norroy, who enjoyed mutually exclusive provincial jurisdictions south and north of the

River Trent, and Garter, who had a somewhat undefined but general jurisdiction, and a higher status than the other two Kings of Arms. These three continue to exist today, with six "ordinary" heralds and four pursuivants. All these officers of arms share an office in London known as the College of Arms, and meet together in a "chapter" to discuss matters of common interest.(5)

Although Scotland also had heralds as early as the fourteenth or fifteenth century, it seems that the surviving records of that period contain little more than fleeting references to their activities; one of these is to Dundee (one of the earliest known heralds to be called by a name of office) who acted as a messenger from the Scottish lords to the English King in 1333. It seems that from relatively early times there was a single principal herald or King of Arms in Scotland, with the name Lyon, who is believed to have joined his armorial functions to the pre-heraldic functions of High Sennachie, or guardian of the royal pedigree. Since at least the middle of the sixteenth century Lyon has been assisted by an officer called Lyon Clerk, who is mentioned in Chapter 3 as Keeper of the Records of Lyon Court. There are also a number of "ordinary" heralds and pursuivants (three of each since 1867).(6)

In medieval times there were a number of lords in all three kingdoms who maintained their own officers of arms, but by the seventeenth century the only remaining "private" heralds were in Scotland and, it seems, in one or two French households. Even today there are a few pursuivants dependant on members of the ancient higher nobility of Scotland. The "heralds extraordinary" sometimes appointed in England nowadays have been said to be the descendants of the old "private" heralds. Extraordinary officers of arms are sometimes appointed in Scotland.(7)

The Constables of France and of England exercised authority over the heralds in the fifteenth century. For example, in 1447 the Constable of France laid down rules of precedence between the heralds and sergeants at arms. The Marshals of France, and the Marshal (later Earl Marshal) of England, who were associated with the respective Constables (especially in the control of aspects of military and chivalric matters), shared in this authority and continued to exercise it after the effective suppression of the Constables, which occurred in England in the early part of the sixteenth century and in France about a century later.

By the sixteenth century the French heralds were no longer under the direct control of the Constable, but had been put under the authority of the Master of the Horse ("Grand Ecuyer"), who was himself originally subordinate to the Constable.

The heraldic authority of the Marshals of France was by the eighteenth century being exercised mainly in relation to appeals from decisions of the Juge d'Armes.(8)

In Scotland the situation was different. It seems that the Constable and the Marischal never had authority over the heralds. There is in fact no intermediate authority between the Sovereign and the Lord Lyon.(9)

In England the Earl Marshal acted in the sixteenth century to reaffirm his authority over the Kings of Arms, who were nominated by him, and laid down a number of rules to be followed by them and by the other heralds. Nevertheless the English heralds made some attempt in the course of the seventeenth century to escape from the control of the Earl Marshal and to act independently of him.

An end was put to all such attempts by a Declaration of Charles II in 1673, confirmed by an Order in Council in 1674, which affirmed the powers of the Earl Marshal as next and immediate Officer under the Sovereign to order all matters touching arms, ensigns of nobility, honour and chivalry, according to the law of arms. Since then the authority of the Earl Marshal over all English heralds has been unquestioned. Although not himself a member of the College of Arms, the Earl Marshal is the head of the heraldic executive in England. He is one of the English Officers of State and, as mentioned in Chapter 3, the judge of the English Court of Chivalry.(10)

The Earl Marshal has for centuries nominated the heralds for appointment by the Sovereign by Letters Patent under the Great Seal. He prescribes rules for them to follow. The Royal Declaration of 1673 and the Order in Council of 1674, which affirmed his powers to order all matters touching arms, ensigns of nobility, honour and chivalry, also affirmed his powers to make rules and ordinances for the regulation of such matters. Subject to the Earl Marshal's control and approval, the heralds may themselves make rules for the ordering of armorial matters in England. It has been stated that the "jurisdiction of the Earl Marshal, coupled with the inherent right of the Kings of Arms to regulate arms, and the power expressly delegated to them by the Sovereign to grant arms, constitute the authority of the officers of arms over all matters of arms".(11)

Attempts were made, first in the sixteenth century, and again between 1660 and 1695, to secure the order and jurisdiction of the College of Arms by Act of Parliament and so provide statutory backing for the activities of the English heralds, but all these attempts were unsuccessful.(12)

The head of the heraldic executive in Scotland is the Lord Lyon King of Arms, who is one of the Scottish Officers of State and, as mentioned in Chapter 3, the judge of Lyon Court. It is the Lord Lyon who appoints the other Scottish heralds.(13)

The authority of the Lord Lyon was originally derived from royal delegation and custom, but it has also been provided with statutory backing by several Acts of Parliament. An Act of the Scottish Parliament of 1592 affirmed various powers of the Lord Lyon and his brother heralds, among which were the powers to "visit" the arms of noblemen, barons and gentlemen, to distinguish these arms with "congruent differences", and to matriculate them in their registers. In 1662 an Act of Parliament referred to the usurping of the chief arms by cadets of families, and ordered that cadets should only bear arms with distinctions which were to be given them by the Lord Lyon; however, this Act was repealed in 1663. In 1672 a further Act of the Scottish Parliament provided that for "the more vigorous prosecution" of the Act of 1592, all "noblemen barons and gentlemen who make use of any arms or signs armorial" were to produce them to Lyon through Lyon Clerk together with information as to their positions in their families, whereupon Lyon might distinguish their arms with "congruent differences" and matriculate them in his registers. Lyon's power to grant arms was confirmed. The only arms which could be borne and used would be the arms matriculated in Lyon's register, which was to be "respected as the true and unrepealable rule of all arms and bearings in Scotland to remain with the Lyon's Office as a public register of the Kingdom."(14)

An Act of the British Parliament of 1867 confirmed that Lyon was to have "the same rights, duties, powers, privileges, and dignities as have heretofore belonged to the Lyon King of Arms in Scotland". This was subject to some minor points, the main ones being that Lyon was to exercise his office himself rather than by deputy, and that in case of necessary absence the Lord President of the Court of Session might commission someone to act for Lyon *ad interim*.(15)

The powers of the Lord Lyon include that of laying down rules if the law of arms is deficient in some respect. It has been stated that "the Court of the Lord Lyon is ... to a certain extent a legislature, in which the laws of arms may be defined, the heralds having voice and vote, the pursuivants voice only".(16)

While the powers of the English and Scottish heralds were increasing in the fifteenth and sixteenth centuries, those of the French heralds were fading away.

The reign of the parcimonious Louis XI was not favourable to the heralds. His successor Charles VIII appointed a "Marshal of Arms" in 1487 to visit all arms borne in the kingdom and to reform abuses, but it seems that these duties were not carried out. In the sixteenth century calls were still made to the heralds to seek out infringements of the laws of arms. For example, it seems that in 1535 Francis I ordered them to carry out a Visitation for the purpose of detecting rich non-nobles who had assumed "timbred" arms or who had usurped the existing arms of noble families. The heralds were not empowered to judge and punish offenders; they were to prosecute the latter before the Royal Courts. However, they could charge an offender to cease his offence and, if he complied, this would make a court action unnecessary.(17)

During the sixteenth and seventeenth centuries the prestige and power of the French heralds continued to decline. At a time when almost all grants of arms in England and Scotland were being made by the Kings of Arms of these countries, the French heralds were unable to make any grants at all. They sometimes served to settle the precise form of arms granted by the King, but even this humbler role seems to have been wholly lost before the eighteenth century. In the 1635 edition of his book, Geliot referred to the heralds as former heroes who had become "almost useless zeroes". There continued to be a "King of Arms" and a dozen heralds in France, but their only surviving duties in the eighteenth century were to attend certain ceremonies and, in the case of the King of Arms, to proclaim wars and peace treaties. In the 1780's proposals were made to revive the other duties and raise the status of the King of Arms, but nothing came of them. The heralds still enjoyed a few privileges, but attempts made by them to persuade the King to attach hereditary nobility to their posts met with failure.(18)

Whereas in earlier times the French Kings of Arms had been elected (with the King's approval) by the other heralds and then formally presented by the Constable to the King who himself crowned the newly elected King of Arms, this procedure had ceased before the seventeenth century. By that time it was the Master of the Horse who nominated them for appointment by the King, administered their oath of office, and could even dismiss them. In spite of the subordination of the officers of arms to the Master of the Horse, this Officer of State does not seem to have taken any part in the administration of heraldic matters.(19)

The ineffectiveness of the French heralds caused the Crown to create new officers to perform certain specific functions. In 1595 Henry IV issued Letters Patent in the form of an Edict, in the general assembly of the Order of the Holy Ghost, by which he appointed the then Historiographer of France to draw up the genealogies and proofs of nobility required for persons who were to be admitted to the Order. Such persons were also required to have been admitted to the older Order of St. Michael. The two Orders were known as the King's Orders ("les Ordres du Roi"), and in consequence the name given to the new post was Genealogist of the King's Orders ("Généalogiste des Ordres du Roi"), which was later abbreviated to King's Genealogist ("Généalogiste du Roi"). The King's Genealogist was later given additional duties; these, like his original functions, involved the study of genealogies rather than arms, but the families concerned were armorial families and some of his documents contain records of their arms.(20)

In 1615 an Edict of Louis XIII created a new armorial authority in the person of a "Juge Général d'Armes de France" or "Juge d'Armes". This authority was constituted quite separately from the Kings of Arms and other heralds, but in some ways the Juge d'Armes was a sort of superior King of Arms. He was appointed by the King on the nomination of the Master of the Horse, and formed part of the latter's Department of the Royal Household. The Master of the Horse administered the oath of office to the Juge d'Armes, but seems to have exercised little control over the armorial activities of the latter. From 1641 until 1790 the post of Juge d'Armes remained in the celebrated d'Hozier family; the first member of this family to be appointed to the post had previously been a herald with the name Toulouse. It had originally been the King's intention that the heralds should be available to advise the Juge d'Armes, but they neglected this opportunity of retaining some of their usefulness and the Juge d'Armes remained the sole effective officer of arms.(21)

The irrelevance of the heralds to armorial matters is illustrated by the fact that when the Armorial Général was being drawn up at the end of the seventeenth century, as described in Chapter 9, the heralds were not given any functions connected therewith, and were completely ignored.

The Juge d'Armes, on the other hand, saw his office abolished, but was compensated by being given the new office of Keeper of the Armorial Général; in 1701 he was restored to the post of Juge d'Armes, and in 1706 his powers were further defined by Order in Council.

According to the Edict in 1615 creating the post of Juge d'Armes, he was to have power to judge armorial errors and persons able to bear arms, and to have jurisdiction in disputes between persons relating to armorial matters. He was to examine and approve the. arms of those who might be ennobled by the King. No "Recherches" (Visitations) of the arms of the nobles were to be carried out without his approval. Appeals from his decisions were to be taken to the Marshals of France.(22)

The Edict of 1701 restoring the post of Juge d'Armes specified that this officer was to enjoy the powers previously attributed to the post, while the Order in Council of 1706 provided that he was to settle future "timbred" arms for registration in the Armorial Général; that, when requested by private citizens, he was to correct arms which had been registered in the Armorial Général but which were erroneous; and that he was to settle officially (by an "Acte de Règlement") the arms of those who might receive Royal grants of nobility, of change of name and arms, or of arms. (23)

It was in virtue of the Order in Council of 1706 that the Juge d'Armes issued "Règlements de Réformation" to persons who applied for the correction of arms which had been described wrongly in the Armorial Général of 1696-1709.(24)

The provision in the Order in Council which forbade the bearing of timbred arms unless they had been approved by the Juge d'Armes and registered the Armorial Général was to remain a dead letter. No timbres were ever included in the arms registered in the Armorial Général, and in any case all registrations therein ceased in 1709.(25)

CHAPTER 5

GRANTS OF ARMS

While there are several earlier instances of a sovereign or a great noble granting, to someone he wished to honour, the right to use some portion of his own arms, it seems that it was not until the second half of the fourteenth century that a formal grant of wholly new arms was made by any sovereign. The first known royal grant of this sort whose contents are recorded appears to be one made in 1389 by Richard II of England to one of his subjects. The grant states that the King has received the grantee into the estate of gentleman ("en l'estat de gentil home") and has made him "Esquier", and wishes him to be known by arms and henceforth to bear certain arms which are blazoned in the grant. A few other English royal grants of nobility and arms are recorded which date from the fifteenth century. Thus in two grants in 1449 Henry VI stated that he ennobled the grantee and, as a sign of this nobility, conferred on him the arms depicted in the grant. Such grants were generally made by Letters Patent under the Great Seal. In some the arms were only depicted, for example in the middle of the document. In others, especially later in the century, the arms were both blazoned and depicted.(1)

The English Kings also made grants of arms in the fifteenth century to some of their French subjects. An example is a grant of Henry VI to one of his subjects in Aquitaine, which conferred nobility on the grantee and, as a sign thereof, also conferred on him certain arms depicted in the grant.(2)

After the granting of arms had become part of the functions of the English Kings of Arms in the course of the fifteenth and sixteenth centuries (as will be described below), grants by English sovereigns became even rarer than they had been. While the sovereign has retained the personal power to make grants of arms, this power has usually been exercised in modern times by means of a Royal Warrant addressed to the Earl Marshal (or directly to the Kings of Arms) ordering that the Kings of Arms

27

should make the actual grant. A similar procedure may be followed when someone's existing arms are to receive an "augmentation of honour". Some Royal Warrants appear to constitute direct grants; even these, however, often include a stipulation that the effect of the grant depends on the arms being exemplified or recorded in the College of Arms. Several royal grants were made to foreigners in the sixteenth and seventeenth centuries, without any reference to the Earl Marshal or to the Kings of Arms (or the College of Arms); the reason may have been that these had authority over Englishmen only. An example is a grant made by Elizabeth I to a Swede in 1583; the Letters Patent (which are in Latin) express the Queen's intention of ennobling the grantee and enabling him to bear arms as a sign of his nobility, and proceed to grant him certain arms.(3)

It is known that grants of arms were made by the French Kings in early times. So far as is known, the first grants of wholly new arms took place in the fifteenth century. Thus, Letters Patent of nobility issued in 1429 by Charles VII in favour of a companion of Joan of Arc also included a grant of ensigns of nobility ("nobilitatis insignia") based on a vision the grantee had had of angels in the sky; accordingly he was granted an azure shield bearing a representation of three angels' heads. In 1441 the same King ennobled two men who had distinguished themselves in battle, and granted them arms. Two woodmen who saved the King from a bear in 1447 are said to have been ennobled, and to have been granted identical arms depicting the bear's paw.(4)

A grant of nobility was not necessarily accompanied by a grant of arms. Until the sixteenth century it seems to have been the King's usual practice to leave it to the new noble to assume arms, for which purpose he might consult the heralds to ensure that his new arms complied with the conventions of heraldry and did not infringe the existing rights of others. It was only for some special reason or as a special mark of favour that a grant of arms was included in the grant of nobility (or followed it, as happened with the arms granted by Louis XI to his favourite, Olivier Le Daim, in 1474).(5)

Letters Patent of the French Kings granting arms were in the form of charters sealed with the Great Seal. In the first half of the fifteenth century the arms were blazoned and depicted; later it was usual not to blazon them but only to depict them, for example in a central area of the document.(6)

In the sixteenth century a grant of nobility might include some generalised reference to arms, as when Henry III stated in certain Letters Patent of ennoblement issued in 1579 that he wished the grantee and his posterity to be free to bear "their accustomed arms" as a sign of their nobility.(7)

Royal grants of arms to non-nobles without a grant of nobility seem to have been very rare; indeed it seems possible that the few which can be found did not include an explicit grant of nobility only because the King had been led to believe that the grantee was already noble. Apart from grants of an "augmentation of honour" to persons who were believed to be already noble, most (perhaps all) royal grants of arms were made as part of, or in consequence of, grants of nobility. Such grants were made to foreigners as well as to Frenchmen. In the seventeenth century the grant of arms might be effected by including in the Letters Patent of ennoblement a statement to the effect that the King permitted, or granted the right to, the grantee and his descendants to bear the arms depicted in the document. If the ennobled person's family had already made use of arms (as was possible, especially in the seventeenth century) these might be depicted in the Letters Patent.(8)

After 1706 the ennobled person was usually directed to obtain a "settlement of arms" from the Juge d'Armes (see below). If the family already had arms, the Letters Patent might state that the ennobled person and his descendants were to be "permitted to bear the ancient arms of their family as shown, painted and depicted in the present Letters and in the Act of Settlement issued by ... the Juge d'Armes ... and attached hereto ..." If new arms were involved the Letters Patent might permit the ennobled person and his descendants "to bear timbred arms as they will be settled and depicted by the ... Juge d'Armes ... and as they will

29

be painted and depicted in these presents to which his Act of Settlement will be attached …"

There were exceptions. For instance, Louis XV issued Letters Patent in 1773 and 1774 confirming the nobility of some of his own natural children and conferring on them arms which were unrelated to the Royal Arms. The King continued to grant augmentations of honour, but he sometimes did this by instructing the Juge d'Armes to issue a "settlement of arms" containing the augmentation.(9)

Presumably the King of Scots, like other sovereigns, made grants of arms in medieval times. He is known to have made such grants in the first half of the sixteenth century. While the King has always continued to have the power to make grants himself, it seems that after the middle of the sixteenth century all grants were in fact made by the Lord Lyon King of Arms, who has been said to stand in place of the King in his armorial jurisdiction. The Sovereign sometimes directs a Royal Warrant to the Lord Lyon to command the latter to assign arms, for example arms to be borne in Scotland by a member of the British Royal Family, or to assign an "augmentation of honour" to a subject in Scotland.

No grant of arms in Scotland can take its full effect until the arms have been matriculated in the Lord Lyon's registers, as by an Act of the Scottish Parliament of 1672 no subject may bear arms unless they have been so registered.(10)

In medieval Europe one of the duties of the heralds was to be aware of the arms borne by the noble men in their provinces. In the fifteenth century heralds took an oath of creation; the oaths of the French and English Kings of Arms required them to ascertain and record the names and arms of the nobles. From about that time, or perhaps somewhat later, the Scottish King of Arms took a similar oath.(11)

Their duty to ascertain and record arms was perhaps the ground from which grew the later practice of the heralds, first to provide more or less official recognition of new arms assumed by their bearers, and then to provide more or less official advice on the choice of such new arms. The French heralds seem never to have got much beyond this stage; there are later references to their having "given" arms to newly ennobled persons at some indeterminate period, but they do not seem to have reached the stage of making formal grants of arms before their general decline set in during the fifteenth century. After that there was no question of their being able to make such grants, although for a time they continued to be available for consultation by persons who wanted to ensure that their arms complied with the rules of heraldry; traces of this activity can be found as late as the early part of the seventeenth century.(12)

The Edict of 1615 which created the office of Juge d'Armes did not give the new officer any power to grant arms of his own motion, but it provided that the arms to be depicted in future Letters Patent of ennoblement must have received the approval of the Juge d'Armes. Moreover, a number of persons bearing assumed arms were able to obtain from the Juge d'Armes a confirmatory document which provided them with evidence of proprietorship, but this facility does not seem to have been widely used.(13)

In the eighteenth century it was unusual for grants of ennoblement to include grants of arms. However, recipients of such grants were directed to obtain what was called a settlement ("Règlement") of arms from the Juge d'Armes. (The necessity for this was laid down by an Order in Council of 1706, which specified that no Letters Patent of ennoblement or of grants of arms were to be issued unless the "Acte de Règlement" of the Juge d'Armes was attached thereto.) As we have seen, the Letters Patent of ennoblement might state that the ennobled person and his descendants were permitted to bear timbred arms which were to be settled by the Juge d'Armes. The Juge d'Armes then issued the settlement, using a form of words which might be along the following lines:"In view of the Letters Patent granted by the King by which His Majesty has ennobled (here followed the name), We, by virtue of the clause in the said Letters which permits the said … and his … descendants to bear timbred arms

31

as they are to be settled by us as Juge d'Armes of the nobility of France and as they are to be depicted in the said Letters to which our Act of Settlement is to be attached ... in accordance with the Order in Council of 9 March 1706, have settled as his arms (here followed the blazon of the arms), the said shield being timbred with a helm in profile furnished with its mantling ..." In addition to being blazoned in the settlement, the arms were depicted both in the middle of the settlement and in the middle of the Letters Patent of ennoblement.(14)

The Order in Council of 1706 was registered in the Cour des Aides and in the Chambre des Comptes, and was therefore considered by these "sovereign" courts as being in force. However, it was not sent for registration in the Parlements and in consequence the latter "sovereign" courts, basing themselves on the principle that they only applied laws registered by themselves, refused at first to register the settlements of arms by the Juge d'Armes which were attached to Letters Patent of ennoblement submitted for registration by these courts. However, they modified their attitude later in the century.(15)

The Juge d'Armes also issued settlements of arms to other persons, noble and non-noble, who presented a request to this effect. (In the case of a noble, this might be someone who had been ennobled otherwise than by Letters Patent, for example by the tenure of an ennobling office.) After the form of the arms had been agreed with the applicant, the Juge d'Armes issued the settlement over his signature and personal seal, using a form of words which might be along the following lines: "We, by virtue of the powers given to us by the Order in Council of 9 March 1706 in our capacity as Juge d'Armes of the nobility of France, which gives us the inspection and ordering of the bearing of arms, have settled as the arms of the said" (here followed the applicant's name and the blazon of the arms, which were also depicted in the middle of the settlement). If the person concerned was noble, the blazon included a description of his helm and mantling, and these were also depicted.(16)

The issuance of settlements of arms by the Juge d'Armes was an exercise of his power to order and regulate the bearing of arms. In France anyone was entitled to bear arms provided he did not usurp those of someone else and provided he did not timbre his arms unless he was noble; all the Juge d'Armes could do was to regulate the exercise of this right, to ensure that the conventions of heraldry were observed and that there was no intentional or unintentional copying of the arms of others. The Juge d'Armes (like the French heralds before him) was never given the power to exercise the King's prerogative of making grants of arms. To put it another way, the Kings of France did not delegate the exercise of their inherent prerogative of granting arms to their subjects.

It was otherwise in England and Scotland. The English Kings of Arms were making formal grants of arms by Letters Patent in the fifteenth century. The legal authority for such grants is not clear. At that period the royal Letters Patent creating the Kings of Arms merely referred in general terms to their liberties, pre-eminences, rights, profits, and so forth, but contained no explicit delegation of the power to create new arms. It was probably still common for new arms to be simply assumed, and it may be that the earliest "grants" from the Kings of Arms amounted to little more than quasi-official records of assumptions of arms. The Ordinances of the Duke of Clarence (who died in 1421) contain certain provisions which indicate that the Kings of Arms could give arms in certain circumstances. However, it seems probable that these provisions were inserted some time after the death of the Duke. At any rate, some of the later fifteenth century grants were worded in a way which appears to imply the existence of a power delegated by the King.(17)

In the early part of the sixteenth century there was a dispute between two of the English Kings of Arms, which so annoyed Henry VIII that he told them that they really derived no power to grant arms from their Letters Patent of creation, and he threatened no longer to allow them to meddle in such matters.(18)

The result might have been to lower the powers and status of the English heralds, and bring them to the condition of the French heralds. However, the King relented, and at last gave the Kings of Arms a formal and express authority to grant arms. As in a Commission of Visitation issued in 1530 in favour of Clarenceux, Letters Patent creating new Clarenceux and Norroy in 1536 explicitly authorised them to grant arms to suitable persons. Garter's position was somewhat anomalous. In 1522 new Statutes of the Order of the Garter referred to his authority to grant arms. In 1539 an agreement among the heralds provided that in future only the provincial Kings of Arms should make grants. It was not until the last years of the sixteenth century that Garter's Letters Patent of creation first contained an explicit authorisation to make grants of arms.(19)

In the latter part of the sixteenth century, and in the seventeenth century, there were disputes as to whether Garter could make grants of arms without reference to the two provincial Kings of Arms. The matter was eventually settled in 1680 by an Order made by the Earl Marshal, which provided that grants to persons in each of the two provinces should be made jointly by Garter and the respective provincial King of Arms. This still applies.(20)

The Earl Marshal's control of the granting of arms had been asserted by him in the sixteenth century, when he had ordered the Kings of Arms not to grant arms without his approval. For a long time this order was partly obeyed (a few grants specified that the Earl Marshal's approval had been obtained), partly circumvented (the order did not forbid the mere confirmation of existing arms without approval, and a number of "confirmations" seem to have been disguised grants), and partly ignored. In 1638 the King's Advocate brought an action in the Court of Chivalry against Norroy, alleging that he had granted arms to someone who was not a gentleman and without a warrant from the Earl Marshal, contrary to the Earl Marshal's decrees and statutes (there is no further information about this case). Since the affirmation of the authority of the Earl Marshal in the Royal Declaration and Order in Council of 1673 and 1674, and the Order made by the Earl Marshal in 1680, the consent of the Earl Marshal has been explicitly recited in all Letters Patent of Arms issued by the Kings of Arms.(21)

While the Earl Marshal's approval is required before a grant of arms can be made by the Kings of Arms, the Earl Marshal does not himself make grants to individuals. There are a few apparent exceptions. Thus in 1673 the Deputy Earl Marshal issued orders which appointed arms to be borne by three persons. The Kings of Arms considered these orders to be invasions of their rights. In 1677 the Deputy Earl Marshal ordered that one of these orders should be expunged from the records of the College of Arms.(22)

For the last three centuries their royal Letters Patent of creation have given the English Kings of Arms power to grant arms to "eminent men", provided the Earl Marshal's approval is first obtained. Throughout that period it has been the practice for memorials (petitions) praying for a grant of arms to be addressed to the Earl Marshal, asking him to direct his warrant to the Kings of Arms. It is the latter who settle the arms to be granted. The grant is in the form of Letters Patent in which the arms are both blazoned and depicted; it is signed by the two appropriate Kings of Arms (sometimes by all three) and sealed with their official seals.(23)

In Scotland, there seems to be no record of a grant of arms by the Lord Lyon before the middle of the sixteenth century. In a grant made in 1567 Lyon states that he "has assigned and assigns" certain arms to the grantee; the whole achievement is depicted in this grant, but only the shield is blazoned.(24)

As late as 1620, the royal Letters Patent creating each Lord Lyon contained only a general reference to the powers of his office, but since 1663 such Letters Patent (which until the reign of Victoria were in Latin) have explicitly conferred the power to grant arms to "virtuous and well-deserving persons" (or "personis virtute praeditis, et de nobis bene meritis"). This power was confirmed to all Lords Lyon by Act of the Scottish Parliament in 1672 (and was subsequently mentioned in Acts of that Parliament relating to individual Lords Lyon, the last such Act being passed in 1707, in the last year of the life of that Parliament).(25)

Petitions praying for a grant of arms are addressed to the Lord Lyon, who may direct a warrant to the Lyon Clerk authorising the latter to prepare the actual grant, but it is the Lord Lyon who settles the arms to be granted. The grant is in the form of Letters Patent in which the arms are both blazoned and depicted; it is signed by the Lord Lyon and sealed with the seal of his office.(26)

Most grants of arms are discretionary or "ministerial" acts, and it is legally within the discretion of the relevant heraldic authority to decide whether to grant arms to a particular person or not, and the authority need give no reason for its decision. This is the situation in England and Scotland. If the Earl Marshal or the Lord Lyon refuses to accede to a petition for a grant of arms, the petitioner has no recourse in law, although he could attempt to obtain a Royal Warrant directing the Earl Marshal or the Lord Lyon to proceed with the grant. Nowadays this would have to be done through the appropriate Secretary of State in either case. Presumably something analogous would have applied in France if the Juge d'Armes had refused to issue a settlement of arms: no doubt it would have been possible to petition the King to order the Juge d'Armes to act. However, the fact that in French law anyone could assume a shield of new arms without any need for a settlement made this an academic point. (In the case of settlements consequent on Letters Patent of ennoblement, the Juge d'Armes had no discretion and was obliged to obey the royal command to settle the arms.)(27)

CHAPTER 6

ASSUMED ARMS

In the post-medieval period, new arms could be created by grant from the Crown or its representatives. Could they be created in any other way? In particular, could a person make up arms for himself? This is the question to be considered now. (We are not concerned with the question whether a particular legal status or qualification is required to make a person fit to bear arms; we assume for the present purpose that if there is some such qualification the person we are now considering has it already.)

There are so many records of bearers of arms in medieval times, and so few records of grants of arms in those times (especially if we disregard the grants by which the grantor did not so much create new arms as give a favoured person a right to use some feature taken from the grantor's existing arms), that we are forced to the conclusion that most medieval arms came into existence by being simply assumed by their first bearers. Nor is there any convincing reason to suppose that such assumptions were unlawful at that time.

The subsequent evolution of the law differed from country to country. We will first consider France, where the medieval freedom to make up one's own arms remained generally undisturbed; then Scotland, where the abolition of this freedom was clearly effected by statute; and finally England, where some commentators claim that this freedom has not yet been wholly abolished in law.

We will preface our remarks by noting that in all three countries it is accepted that, in law, the enjoyment of a right since "time immemorial" (or "before the limits of legal memory") makes that right secure and indefeasible. (This may be called the first type of prescription.) In the absence of positive proof that the right was enjoyed since "time immemorial", a court may nevertheless be prepared to presume that the right was so enjoyed if there is positive proof of enjoyment over a substantial period and if there is no proof that the right was not enjoyed before the start of that period.

In application of this principle, enjoyment of arms (actual or presumed) since time immemorial establishes a secure right to those arms in all three countries.(1)

Enjoyment over a substantial period which is proved not to have existed before the start of that period is clearly not enjoyment since "time immemorial", and therefore cannot benefit from the rules about what we have called the first type of prescription. However, in some parts of the law there are special rules (either statutory or recognised by the courts) which provide that use over a certain time span is a sufficient condition to render a right secure, irrespective of whether the right can be proved not to have existed before that time span began. (This may be called the second type of prescription.)

Is the law of arms one of the parts of the law where this second type of prescription applies? The answer to this question seems to be positive in France, negative in Scotland (since the seventeenth century), and not wholly certain in England.

While there were some French commentators of the seventeenth and eighteenth centuries who took the view that it was unlawful to bear arms without the Crown's permission, this was mere wishful thinking. There are practically no signs of any attempt by the royal authority to restrict new arms to those granted or approved by that authority. Although, as the King himself had stated, in a document of 1474 relating to someone he had ennobled and to whom he was now granting arms, it was "necessary for him to have them as a sign and demonstration of the said state of nobility", such a grant of arms to an ennobled person, or accompanying an ennoblement, remained quite exceptional until the sixteenth century, and the normal practice was to leave it to the new noble to assume arms with or without the advice of a herald.(2)

In a book published in 1746 relating to the history of Brittany, it is mentioned that in 1536 the King prohibited "all his subjects" from assuming arms without his permission. A modern commentator has suggested that if this prohibition was really made it may have been limited to Brittany. Another hypothesis which comes to mind is that the author of the book may have been thinking of the Ordinance of 1556 which is mentioned in Chapter 7; by 1746 there were many who believed that this local and temporary law was a subsisting general law.(3)

During the few years (1696-1709) in which the laws relating to the Armorial Général (discussed in Chapter 9) were in force, it was unlawful to bear arms unless they had been registered, but anyone was free to make up new arms and register them. The Royal Declaration of 1760 (which is also discussed in Chapter 9) purported to institute compulsory registration of arms, but it did not become law.

An Order in Council of 1706 defining the powers of the Juge d'Armes seems to have laid down that no-one was to bear timbred arms (that is, arms surmounted by a helm or coronet) unless they had been settled by the Juge d'Armes and registered in the Armorial Général. In fact no timbred arms were ever registered in the Armorial Général, which in any case was closed in 1709. While those who were ennobled by Royal Letters Patent in the eighteenth century did usually obtain settlements of timbred arms from the Juge d'Armes, many of those who acquired nobility in other ways did not do so (although some did).(4)

With the closing of the Armorial Général, the ancient customs recovered their force. Anyone could make up a shield of arms for himself (provided he did not infringe the prior right of another person). Alternatively he could bear the ancient arms of his family (if any), or arms registered by his family in the Armorial Général (in which there are instances of up to five different arms being registered in the names of different members of a single family). If he wished, he could apply to the Juge d'Armes to settle his arms officially; this was the usual procedure if he was the recipient of Royal Letters Patent of ennoblement.(5)

While the use of new arms created rights therein, these did not constitute a defence against legal action by a different family which could prove that it had borne the same arms since an earlier date. In such circumstances a court might order the later user to cease using the arms. However, it seems that the longer the period of concurrent use the more willing a court would be to decide that a slight difference in the arms was sufficient to justify continued use. When the great family of Créqui (or a wild cherry tree eradicated gules) cited a Lejeune family (gules a wild cherry tree couped or) before the Juge d'Armes in the eighteenth century, the fact that the Lejeune family could prove that it had borne its arms for more than a century encouraged the Juge d'Armes to reject the objections against these arms.(6)

One case is remarkable in that it ended with the Royal Council confirming a minor noble family in the possession of what was a differenced version of the Royal Arms. A Norman family named Brossard, which could prove nobility since at least the early part of the fifteenth century, generally bore azure three fleurs de lys or debruised by a bend or bendlet or bend sinister argent or gules. These arms were challenged at various times, and in 1663 a judgment of the Cour des Aides of Normandy ordered the members of this family (or some of them) to alter the tinctures of their arms, so that the field became gules, the fleur de lys argent and the bend sinister also argent. In the course of the nobiliary survey of 1666 etc., (which is discussed in Chapter 9), some members of the family gave in the old arms while others gave in the new version. Questions were again raised. Thirty years later, the officials of the Armorial Général (who had been instructed not to register any arms containing a fleur de lys or on an azure field unless good authority was demonstrated, and who often referred such cases to central authority) generally insisted on registering different arms (for example, azure a bend argent). The disputes dragged on. Eventually, there was a final decision by the highest possible authority. On evidence that for over two centuries the Brossard family had borne azure three fleurs de lys or, debruised by a bend or baston argent, the Juge d'Armes felt bound to advise the Crown that the family could not be deprived of these arms, and in 1786 an Order in Council finally confirmed this family in the possession of these arms.(7)

In Scotland, it does not seem to have been suggested that arms which were borne in the fifteenth century, and which seem to have been assumed at that time, were in any way unlawful. Indeed, it seems to be accepted that, at least until 1592, it was possible to develop rights in new arms by long-continued (but not necessarily immemorial) use.(8)

No such possibility exists since the Acts of the Scottish Parliament of 1592 and 1672 which forbade the bearing of any arms unless they had been matriculated by the Lord Lyon. He will matriculate arms which have been granted or confirmed, and arms which have not been proved to have been granted or confirmed but which are proved to have been used before 1672 (the latter will be formally confirmed by Lyon before being matriculated). Mere use of arms after 1672 creates no rights therein.(9)

In England the legal position has not been made as clear as in Scotland, and there is a dispute among commentators as to whether a right to arms can even now be established by what we have called the second type of prescription, that is, use over a period which does not amount to proof or even to a presumption of use since "time immemorial".(10)

The only thing in the nature of a statute which seems relevant to this dispute is a proclamation or direction issued by Henry V in 1417. The import of this proclamation is itself part of the dispute. The proclamation applied to those who were to form part of an army which was to accompany the King to France. It forbade them to assume arms, but made an exception for those who had fought at Agincourt in 1415. Some have seen this proclamation as constituting an isolated or exceptional rule; others, as an application of a more general law. The reference to Agincourt may provide a clue as to the King's intentions. It was believed, and was probably true, that the King had accepted that all who had fought with him at Agincourt had been ennobled thereby. It seems to have been the view of Upton, not many years after the proclamation of 1417, that those who had become noble, and only they, could assume arms (this point is considered in Chapter 12). Perhaps the proclamation was only intended to forestall a mass claim to nobility and its insignia by all who were to take part in the next campaign in France, and to make it clear that what might be called the Agincourt privilege was limited to that battle.(11)

Another royal command, issued more than a century after that of Henry V, seems of somewhat clearer import. In his Letters Patent of 1530 relating to a Visitation about to be carried out by one of the Kings of Arms, Henry VIII instructed the latter to reform "arms devised without authority".(12)

Does this not seem clear enough? The King does not admit that a man can make up arms for himself. Perhaps, after all, this is also how the proclamation of Henry V is to be understood. But doubts exist. What "authority" did the King have in mind? Can a rule of law be founded merely on this oblique reference?

When we look for a clear expression of the law in the cases decided by the Court of Chivalry, we find that the available records provide material which is significant but perhaps not conclusive.

In the seventeenth century a number of persons were prosecuted in the Court of Chivalry for the unlawful bearing of arms. The cases in which the alleged offence was usurping the arms of another family are not relevant. However, there were some cases relating to the assumption of new arms. In a number of these cases the court's judgment was against the defendant, or at least the defendant voluntarily submitted and acknowledged that he was not entitled to the arms. Unfortunately there is no record of the reasoning of the court, and therefore no direct record of the rule of law applied by the court. However, on the basis of the pleadings of the parties, it has been persuasively argued by Mr

Squibb that the court must have accepted that a right to arms could be derived only from a grant or from birth.(13)

If this is accepted, then all officially accepted rights must fall into one of these two categories. Prescriptive rights of what we have called the first type (dating in fact or by presumption from "time immemorial") must fall into the second category. As for prescriptive rights of the second type (dating only from a time which can be proved to be more recent than "time immemorial"), they too must fall into the second category — that is, if rights of this type can exist in the English law of arms.

It is a fact that among the officially accepted rights to arms are some which were recognised by the Kings of Arms or their deputies during the Visitations carried out in the sixteenth and seventeenth centuries, such recognition being based on proved periods of use which might be as short as a century; indeed, it appears that proved use over a period of only sixty years might be sufficient.(14)

This fact is interpreted by those who say that only the first type of prescription is possible as showing that such a period was what was then needed to found a presumption of use from "time immemorial". Others say that such a short period as sixty years cannot have been thought by the Kings of Arms to found such a presumption, and that this means that no such presumption is necessary or, in other words, that the second type of prescription is possible.(15)

In the only reported case decided by the Court of Chivalry since 1737, the "Manchester" case heard in 1954 in which the full judgment was issued in 1955, that judgment contained a reference to the right to bear arms being "conferred by a direct grant or by descent from an ancestor to whom the arms had been originally granted", but the words after "or" are an obiter dictum as this point had not been argued and was irrelevant to the decision in that case, where the arms in issue had been granted to the plaintiff.(16)

43

Modern English Kings of Arms are understood to take the view that the second type of prescription is not possible. It has been their practice, since at least the nineteenth century, to refuse to acknowledge or confirm any previously unrecorded arms which are presented to them, however long may be the period during which the arms have been borne. The most they will do is to grant or confirm a differenced version of the arms.(17)

CHAPTER 7

TRANSMISSION

Arms were created by the feudal society of the Middle Ages, and it was natural that they should devolve in the same way as other feudal heritage. An early general custom was that they normally descended from father to son. Other modes of devolution were available, especially when there were no sons. There was a tendancy for a man's arms to follow his property or his other dignities, so that if these passed for some reason to a junior heir male or through a female heir then the arms might follow the same path. With the passage of time and with the increasing control exercised over arms and other dignities by the Crown., more precise rules came to govern the devolution of arms in each country. Most of these rules were in force by the sixteenth or seventeenth century.

One self-evident rule is that if the arms are created by Letters Patent or other granting document, and if that document contains provisions as to the devolution of the arms (the "destination" or the "limitation"), then effect must be given to these provisions. Such provisions may for example specify that the arms are to devolve on heirs male of the body, or heirs general of the body, or heirs male (not necessarily of the body), etc., of the grantee or of some specified person.

More unusual provisions are sometimes found, as in an English grant of arms of 1708 which limited the devolution of the arms to those who were to enjoy the grantee's real estate after his death.(1)

If the arms are simply assumed by their first bearers (as is true of most ancient arms in all countries, and of most modern arms in France), or if the arms are created by documents which are silent as to their devolution or which contain general references to "descendants" or "posterity" (in French documents often "posterity male and female") then the rules vary from country to country.

Before considering some of these rules, the point should be made that it is (or was) the case in all three countries that any given arms can have only one holder at a time. By "holder" is meant a person having both the right to use the arms and the right to transmit the arms. Other persons may have the first of these two rights. For example, it is a wife's privilege to use her husband's arms if she wishes. An unmarried daughter can use her father's arms (what happens if she marries is discussed in Chapter 10). Other members of the family are entitled, at most, only to modified ("differenced") versions of the arms, as discussed in Chapter 8.

In medieval England it seems to have been assumed that the rules as to the inheritance of arms were at least partly similar to those governing the devolution of other ancient dignities such as baronies by writ. That this was so in the fifteenth century is suggested by the only English judicial decision on the devolution of arms, the judgment of the Court of Chivalry in 1410 in the case of Grey v. Hastings. This judgment established that if a man had children by two marriages and his arms were inherited by his son by the first marriage then, if that son's issue became extinct, the next heir was a daughter by the first marriage in preference to a son by the second marriage, so that the latter could only bear a differenced version of the arms. (It has been pointed out that this decision accorded with the English common law rules of inheritance of property, which gave preference to relations of the whole blood over those of the half blood).

The Court of Chivalry did not have jurisdiction over baronies by writ but, acting on the assumption that the rule the court had applied to arms was also applicable to such baronies, the victor in the Grey v. Hastings case, to whom the court had confirmed the undifferenced arms of Hastings, took the style of Lord Hastings, a style which was allowed in 1484 to his grandson when the latter was confirmed by the King in the Earldom of Kent. However, more than three centuries later (in 1841), the House of Lords (which decides itself whether claimants to a seat therein are so entitled) came to a decision whose effect was that it was the descendant of the loser in the Grey v. Hastings case who was accepted as being entitled to the barony of Hastings.(2)

On this basis, it appears either that the decision in Grey v. Hastings was wrong, or that the law changed between 1410 and 1841, or that different rules govern the devolution of arms and the devolution of baronies by writ.

It has been pointed out that the judgment in Grey v. Hastings seems to show that in England arms could descend to the heir general rather than the heir male.(3)

Several instances are known of a female heir transmitting her arms to her issue, who bore them either combined with her husband's arms (usually in a quarterly shield) or alone as their whole arms.(4)

When a man had no sons but several daughters all of whom had issue, it seems that in medieval times it was the eldest daughter who was alone entitled to transmit her father's arms, whole and undifferenced (especially if she also transmitted the principal lands and other dignities of her father). Later, and apparently as a consequence of the development of the modern doctrine of abeyance in connection with the ancient English dignities of baronies by writ, a partly similar doctrine came into existence in English heraldry. In baronies by writ, the doctrine of abeyance means that, in the absence of a son, all daughters share equally in the right to the barony, but such right remains in abeyance unless and until the Crown chooses to nominate one of the daughters to occupy the barony. In heraldry, the partly similar doctrine means that, in the absence of a son, all of a man's daughters have the right to transmit his arms to their issue. However, in modern England this right remains latent in the case of a daughter who marries a man who has no arms of his own, as the English heralds have imposed a rule that (unless a special Royal Licence is obtained), no heiress can transmit her father's arms to her issue except as a quartering in a shield which also contains her husband's arms.(5)

The first thing to be said about the transmission of arms in Scottish heraldry is that a much closer and more continuous control has been exercised there than in other heraldic systems. This is mainly because of the 1672 Act of the Scottish Parliament, which gave the Lord Lyon effective means to control the transmission of arms, since such transmission is subject to judicial matriculation proceedings before the Lord Lyon. In such proceedings the Lord Lyon can ensure that the Scottish rules of devolution are observed. At the same time he can exercise his judicial discretion as to the applicability of the rules in particular circumstances; this gives the system some flexibility.

According to a famous Scottish jurist of the seventeenth century, it was the law that, in the absence of sons, the eldest daughter as eldest heir portioner (female co-heir) inherited her father's arms and transmitted them (whole and unquartered) to her issue if she married a man who himself took her name and her arms. In spite of some confusing statements or decisions by certain Lords Lyon or their deputes, especially in the early part of the nineteenth century, the old Scottish preference for a direct female heir over an indirect male heir has been maintained and has been confirmed by modern decisions of the Lord Lyon. The views of the seventeenth century jurist have been approved not only in Lyon Court but also in the Court of Session.(6)

It is to be emphasised that the ability to transmit the arms unquartered depends on retaining the name. If the daughters all lose their name when they marry, thus in effect leaving their paternal family for the families of their husbands, then all inherit equally, and each can transmit her father's arms to her issue only as a quartering.(7)

The general rules applicable to the transmission of Scottish arms from one holder to the next are analogous to those governing succession to other ancient Scottish dignities. Thus, in the absence of a special destination in the Letters Patent granting the

48

arms or in a subsequent matriculation, the normal rule is that the heir of line succeeds. (The heir of line is the eldest son of the previous holder or, failing sons, the eldest daughter; if the holder has no issue the heir of line is the holder's senior uncle or, failing uncles, senior aunt.)(8)

There is (as already indicated) a close association between the arms and the name, and failure to retain the name usually results in the right to the arms passing to the next heir. Thus, if the heir of line is a woman, she forfeits her rights as heir if she and her heirs take her husband's name. If the rights of an eldest daughter are lost in this way, they may pass to her next sister, and so on.(9)

The ability of a holder of Scottish arms to transmit them is not affected by the armorial status of the holder's spouse. For example, if a woman is the holder of the arms, she can transmit them to her issue whether her husband has arms of his own or not; the only requirement is that her issue must keep her name. If the spouse of a holder of arms is armigerous, then in some circumstances this may result in a quartered coat for the issue of the marriage, but it is preferred to avoid this if possible, either by ignoring one of the arms, or by arranging for one name and its associated arms to pass to one child, and the other name and its associated arms to pass to another child.(10)

If a woman becomes the holder of the arms, and if she has sisters, then these sisters are junior heirs portioners (co-heirs) and as such they may transmit the arms, not as whole and unquartered arms, but quartered with their husbands' arms, the latter occupying the principal quarters. In such cases these junior heirs portioners normally take their husbands' names. However, it is open to them to remain within the family into which they were born, by matriculating differenced versions of the holder's arms and transmitting these, together with their name, to their own heirs (their husbands' names and arms being ignored).(11)

In Scottish heraldry quarterly shields of arms may come into being in various ways. Often, the first quarter contains the paternal arms, and the other quarters contain the arms of various heiresses from whom the holder is descended. (This is somewhat analogous to English practice, except that the modern English practice by which a quartering for an heiress can be included only if quarterings for all "intermediate" heiresses are also included, is not observed in Scotland.) Sometimes the maternal arms appear in the first quarter and the paternal arms (if present) appear in another quarter; this may indicate that the bearer represents his mother's family, in which case he will normally bear her name. Sometimes a quartering denotes what is not a blood relationship but the representation of a feudal lordship or an hereditary office; this occurs but rarely in England. While in Scotland an inescutcheon is relatively seldom used to contain the arms of an heiress wife (which is its normal function in England) it has sometimes been used to contain the paternal arms placed over a shield occupied by quarterings representing heiresses or fiefs.(12)

The laws of armorial transmission in France were generally based on a strong preference for male heirs. The "Salic" law, brought into operation to help prevent the French Crown from devolving through possible female heirs in the fourteenth century, came to be considered so fundamental a part of the constitution that its effects spread first to the transmission of nobility and then to the transmission of arms. In France (as elsewhere) a woman could use her paternal arms, but she could not normally transmit them to her issue, even if she had no brothers. The general rule was that arms devolved on the male heir, however remote.

This rule might be moderated in practice in the following way. If a family, or at least an independant branch, was extinct in the male line or was about to become so, the last male or males of the family might cause the family name and arms to pass to a suitable person, for example the husband of the daughter of one of the last males; or a descendant in a female line, for example the son of a daughter of the family, might assume the arms (with or without the name). This last procedure was known as a "Relèvement d'Armoiries".(13)

In these conditions, arms could be transmitted through a woman, who performed the function of a heraldic heiress. If these

conditions did not apply it seems that it was not lawful for arms
to be transmitted through a woman unless special permission was
obtained from the Crown.

Someone to whom arms were transmitted through a woman
might quarter them with his paternal arms. Often, arms taken up
in this way were borne as the principal arms, being placed either
in the principal quarters of a quarterly shield, or in an
inescutcheon, while the paternal arms were relegated to a
secondary position. Sometimes the arms raised up from
extinction were borne alone, the paternal arms being wholly
disused.(14)

If an "heiress" and her husband had several children, and if it was
desired to perpetuate the arms of the "heiress" and of her
husband separately, then one arms might go to one of the
children and the other arms to another of the children; the names
might also be perpetuated in the same way.(15)

Not only could a woman who was heiress of a family transmit the
arms of that family as a quartering to her issue, but also she could
thus transmit, not her paternal arms, but the arms of a family
which had come to her family through an heiress. For example, if
the heiress of Family A married into Family B, and in a later
generation the heiress of Family B (descended from the heiress of
Family A) married into Family C, the descendants of this
marriage might bear the arms of Family A, either alone or
quartered with those of Family C, there being no obligation on
them to include a quartering of the arms of Family B. (It has been
indicated above that this sort of thing is possible in Scotland; and
it was also possible in fifteenth century England, but is nowadays
said not to be permissible.)(16)

The rule that French arms could not devolve through a woman
except in the circumstances described above was not considered
to be broken by persons who displayed shields which included as
subsidiary quarterings arms to which they had no legal right but
which symbolised alliances. Thus a man might use a shield
containing quarterings of the arms of the families of his wife, his

mother, his grandmother, etc., even if none of them was an heiress. The use of these quarterings was generally only temporary, and was subject to variation in each generation. In such cases it was only the paternal arms which were displayed as of right; they appeared either in the principal quarter or, quite often, on an inescutcheon.(17)

The influence of the Salic law made itself felt less, or later, in some parts of France. In Champagne it was the custom, down at least to the sixteenth century, for the sons of non-noble fathers and noble mothers to consider themselves noble. In Franche-Comté which retained its customary laws when it became part of the Kingdom of France in the seventeenth century, the same custom seems to have applied. In later times it was thought necessary to obtain formal Letters Patent from the King to confirm nobility inherited in this way.

Analogous rules applied to the inheritance of arms in those provinces, as was confirmed for example in a judgment of the Parlement of Paris in 1599, which confirmed the right of a man to bear the name and arms of his mother. The heraldic rights of women in those territories were somewhat similar to those of men. The local laws of some parts of Champagne, as codified in 1494, provided explicitly that, in the absence of sons, the eldest daughter was alone entitled to the name and to the (undifferenced) arms, although other aspects of the paternal property might be shared among all the daughters. The analogy between this mode of inheritance and the transmission of Scottish arms through an eldest daughter has been remarked upon by a late Lord Lyon.(18)

From the sixteenth century onwards some lawyers propounded the view that the taking of arms which had been those of another family (even arms inherited through an heiress) should be subject to a formal approval by the King, especially if these arms were to be borne alone or as the principal arms (that is in an inescutcheon or in the first quarter of a quarterly shield). The only enactment used to support this contention was an Ordinance of 1556 which forbade changes of name and arms without royal permission; but although some later jurists supposed that it was a general law, it has been shown that the Ordinance was of only local and temporary effect, being applicable only to Normandy, and being abrogated only a few months after its enactment. Changes of arms only (or even of both arms and name) continued to be made, especially by nobles taking up those derived from extinct families from which they descended in a female line. Specific approval for such changes was sometimes obtained from the Crown. In other instances the courts referred with approval to such changes in the course of litigation. Many changes were never the subject of any formal official cognisance.(19)

The practice of taking up the arms of extinct families ("Relèvements d'Armoiries") could eventually lead to confusion in certain families, whose members might end by not knowing what were the real arms of their paternal ancestors. In one family, the discovery in the seventeenth century of a marriage contract of the fifteenth century brought to light the fact that the arms the family was using were those of a maternal ancestor. At the time the contract was made, there still existed a senior branch of the husband's family, while it was apparently the case that the wife's family had died out or was expected to do so. The contract stipulated that the children of the marriage were to bear the names of both families but the arms of the wife's family, alone and unquartered; however, it also provided that if the senior branch of the husband's family were to die out, the eldest son of the marriage was to bear the arms of both families quartered. In the course of time a situation arose in which the members of the family bore only one name and only one arms, the name being that of the husband and the arms being those of the wife! It was now felt to be desirable to revive the paternal arms which had long been abandoned. It was decided to seek royal approval for this revival, such approval being particularly desirable as the arms to be revived closely resembled the royal arms, since they were azure three fleurs de lys argent. Royal Letters Patent of 1664 permitted the members of the family to bear both names and to quarter both arms. In general, such royal approval was not considered to be necessary when a family merely revived the arms (and perhaps also the name) which it had originally borne but which it had later replaced by others.(20)

It is possible for arms to be transmitted otherwise than by inheritance. In early times this could be done by a private transaction, embodied for example in a deed of conveyance, but increasing control of armorial matters by the Crown eventually led to a requirement being imposed that the Crown's approval be obtained. This is true of England and Scotland, though perhaps not of France, where private conveyances of arms without prior royal approval continued to be effective in certain conditions until the Revolution.

In England, private conveyances of arms appear to have been effective as late as the fifteenth century. In some (but not all) cases the conveyance of arms accompanied or followed a conveyance of the land whose owners had used the arms.(21)

Somewhat different from a direct conveyance of certain arms was an authorisation granted to a stranger in blood to use a more or less differenced version of the arms. By the seventeenth century it was felt to be necessary, or at least desirable, to obtain the approval of the Crown or its representative, a King of Arms. When Lord Townshend authorised Sir Robert Agborough to use the name of Townshend (by which he had long been known) and to bear a differenced version of the arms of Townshend, he stipulated that the differences should be settled by Garter. Accordingly Garter issued Letters Patent in 1663 by which he granted and confirmed to "the said Sir Robert Agborough by the name and title of Sir Robert Townshend Knt" arms which were the same as those of Lord Townshend except in that the chevron became engrailed and the tincture of the accompanying escallops was changed from argent to ermine.(22)

In modern England it seems that no right in any arms can be transmitted otherwise than by inheritance, unless the Letters Patent creating the arms specify otherwise, or unless a Royal Licence is obtained. The usual reason for such a licence is to give effect to a "name and arms" clause in a will or other settlement of property, but the Crown is prepared to grant such licences on other grounds, provided it is convinced that there are good reasons for allowing the arms (usually accompanied by the name) to be taken by the beneficiary. Royal Licences are nowadays generally granted on the advice of the Home Secretary, and are usually addressed to the Earl Marshal who then authorises the Kings of Arms to give effect thereto, usually by means of their Letters Patent exemplifying the arms in favour of the beneficiary.(23)

In early times English dignities such as peerages could be resigned into the Crown's hands for conferral on someone else. This presumably applied to arms. The resignation and re-grant of peerages ceased in the seventeenth century, and since then the English Crown has not had the power to alter the limitation (destination) even of dignities created by itself. It is consistent with this modern principle that arms cannot be diverted from the course of transmission specified in the grant. The grant of Royal Licences is perhaps not necessarily inconsistent with this (even when other branches of the original family remain), especially now that the rule prohibiting more than one holder of identical arms seems to be unenforced; it appears that the effect of the Royal Licence is not to deprive anyone of any arms, but only to increase the number of those who bear the arms.(24)

It was possible to resign a Scottish feudal dignity to the Crown *in favorem* of someone else or to nominate a successor to such a dignity. In both cases the Crown's approval was necessary. It has been suggested that, following the Treaty (Act) of Union of 1706, Scottish peerages may no longer be treated in this way. Whatever the truth of that suggestion, Scottish arms continue to be subject to such procedures, with the Lord Lyon acting on behalf of the Crown. Accordingly a holder of arms may apply to the Lord Lyon to divert or alter the destination of his arms, irrespective of the provisions in the original grant of arms. The Lord Lyon, if he decides to accede to the application, may do so by his Letters Patent or, more usually, by re-matriculating the arms with an appropriate new destination. There is no need for a Royal Licence, and such licences are never used in Scotland.(25)

In general no alteration will be allowed if it would result in separating the arms from the name; in other words the new holder must already have, or must take, the name which has been associated with the arms. Separating the arms from the blood (such as a settlement of the undifferenced arms on an adopted child) is strongly discouraged. Evidence that a proposed alteration is desirable in the general interest of the family may be required before the Lord Lyon is prepared to act.

The possession by a junior branch of the lands which were historically associated with the main stem of a family is a factor which will encourage the Lord Lyon to view favourably a request that the arms of the head of the family should pass to that branch, which will thereupon itself become the main stem. Since Scottish arms can have only one holder, any heir of what was formerly the main stem but is now only a cadet line (in terms of heraldic status) is obliged to matriculate a differenced version, like any other cadet of the family.(26)

In France, straightforward sales of land with arms annexed were possible as late as the sixteenth century.(27)

Until the Revolution, dispositions of property on condition that the disponee took the name and arms of the disposer, remained common. It was generally necessary for the disposer to be the last male of his family or at least for it to be clear that the family, or the branch which he represented, was about to die out; if there were other males who were likely to keep the family going, then it was not in his power to dispose of the family name and arms. If it was thought that the family was likely to become extinct, but this was not certain, the head of the family could make a disposition conditional on actual extinction taking place.(28)

Dispositions of property could be enforced only if any conditions specified in the dispositions were complied with. This applied for example to "name and arms" clauses. Several cases were litigated before the Bailiwick or Seneschalcy courts and the Parlements, in which such clauses were construed and applied.(29)

From about the sixteenth century it was felt by a number of lawyers that it might be desirable to obtain explicit royal approval of dispositions involving names or arms so as to ensure that they were fully effective. This was encouraged by the attitude of the Crown, which used terminology in some Letters Patent granted to confirm certain specific cases which suggested that the power to approve such changes of name or arms was part of the royal prerogative. However, there seems to have been no relevant enactment (except for the short-lived Ordinance of 1556 already mentioned), and until the Revolution dispositions of names and arms continued to be made either with or without specific royal approval. Some of the latter dispositions came before the Parlements in the course of litigation and were enforced by these courts.(30)

It should be pointed out that in the sixteenth and seventeenth centuries there were some judgments of the Parlements which condemned persons who had changed their names without permission, but it seems that the offence lay in the purpose of the change, which was to facilitate fraud or usurpation of nobility, and that mere change of name without evil intent was not punishable.(31)

Processes of inheritance, conveyance and grant might result in more than one arms falling to a single person. In early times such a person was free to select one for his use, or to use them all independently of each other, or to combine some or all of them in a quarterly shield. In France this remained true in principle. This is also the case in Scotland, where a person may for example be granted one coat, and inherit another. If the destinations applicable to the two coats are different, they may devolve along different paths after that person's death. For example, if one destination is to descendants and the other is to heirs male, and if the person dies leaving no son but a daughter and a brother, the first coat will go to the daughter and the second will go to the brother.(32)

Post-medieval English Kings of Arms have taken the view that a man could have only one personal coat of arms. This led them to refuse to grant arms to anyone who was already entitled to arms, unless the grant recited that the new arms were to be borne in lieu of the earlier arms. However, it is now felt that existing arms are not so easily extinguished, and persons already entitled to arms may now receive grants of English arms without any reference being made to their existing arms.(33)

CHAPTER 8

DIFFERENCING

In medieval times a principle was developed that a particular coat of arms should be the appanage of only one person at a time, and that others, even members of that person's family, should use other arms. This was encouraged by considerations of convenience, which incited different members of a family who might appear at the same place (for example in the field of battle or in a tournament) or who might be holders of different fiefs and have different followings, to identify themselves by means of different arms. On the other hand an opposite tendancy was encouraged by the strong family feelings of the time. These conflicting tendancies were reconciled by a practice in which all members of the family had arms which were sufficiently different to indicate that they belonged to different individuals, yet sufficiently similar to show that these individuals were closely related to one another. Those members of families who were unable to lead an independant existence or to transmit their arms (children and most women) had no need to follow this practice, and generally did not do so.

It was the usual practice for successive "heads" of a family to use the same arms, and for the cadets of the family to use "differenced" versions of these basic arms. From being a conventional practice this became a legal requirement, enforceable by legal action, as we shall see.

In more recent times, when arms had ceased to be the principal means of identifying individuals in war and peace, the utility of differencing within each family was much reduced. The legal requirement remained, but the practice of differencing came to be largely abandoned, except where the heraldic authority was able and willing to enforce it.

While various methods of differencing were developed in medieval times, there was little national variation in the use of the various methods.(1)

The method of differencing which eventually became most common was to leave unaltered the tincture of the field and the nature, number, disposition and tincture of the charges of the "basic" arms, but to add a further charge which would distinguish the differenced arms while preserving a general similarity of character with the "basic" arms. A charge added for this purpose is termed a "brisure" (or a "difference", or a "mark of cadency"). Most of the charges which came to be used as brisures had already been used as ordinary charges; some continued to be used in both ways while others ceased to be used except as brisures.(2)

The most common brisures in medieval France, England and Scotland were the label, the bordure and the bend or its diminutive the cotise or bendlet.(3)

The label came in the course of time to be regarded in England as the brisure of the eldest son (other sons use it only if they are members of the Royal Family). In Scotland the label seems to have become associated with eldest sons at an early date, although this was not an invariable rule. Then followed a period in which the label seems to have been little used in Scotland. Later it was revived for use either as the mark of the eldest son, or as a permanent feature of the arms of the line of a heraldic heir from whom the principal arms have been diverted as described in Chapter 7. In France the label was a widely used brisure. It was not necessarily associated with the eldest son, as is shown by the practice of the Royal Family. The King's eldest son did not need to use a brisure since, as Dauphin, he quartered the King's Arms with those of Dauphiny, which constituted an adequate difference. This made it possible for the King's second son to bear his father's arms with a plain silver label which became hereditary in the line of the Dukes of Orleans. This in turn caused the label to be considered to be an appropriate brisure for the second son in other French families.(4)

The widely used bordure was the subject of explicit royal approval for differencing the arms of cousins. This was in the final judgment pronounced by Richard II in 1390 in the Scrope v. Grosvenor case (the King also stated that a bordure was not a sufficient distinction between the arms of persons who were strangers in blood). In the post-medieval period the use of the bordure as a brisure declined in England and in France, but in Scotland its use for this purpose has been maintained and somewhat systematised.(5)

The bend and certain other large ordinaries which have been used as brisures tend to overpower the other charges in their visual effect, and consequently to change the character of the arms. For this reason the bend, which was commonly used as a brisure in France in medieval times, and the chevron and the fess, which were commonly used for the same purpose in Scotland between the fifteenth and seventeenth centuries, declined in popularity as brisures. They may still be used in appropriate cases; for example a basic shield bearing three identical charges may be suitably differenced by a fess or a chevron without its general character being destroyed.(6)

There were medieval examples of the use of very small brisures which had very little effect on the overall character of the arms - so little, in some cases, as to jeopardise one of the purposes of the use of brisures, that of adequately differencing the arms. These small brisures may have been the forerunners of the later small brisures known as "minor marks of cadency" or simply "cadency marks".(7)

The theory of the use of these minor cadency marks was developed as early as the sixteenth century by a number of writers on heraldry. They assigned a particular mark to the eldest son during his father's lifetime (thereafter he inherited his father's undifferenced arms), another mark to the second son, another to the third, and so on. The descendants of each son were to place their own marks on that of their father so that, in theory, there might be four or five marks one above the other (complete obliteration of one mark by the next was avoided by making the marks successively smaller). The mark of the eldest son was the label: this was consistent with former practice. The marks of the other sons (a crescent for the second son, a mullet for the third, a martlet for the fourth etc) had already been used as ordinary charges or even as brisures (but not in this systematical way); as used in accordance with the new system they were generally much smaller than when used as ordinary charges. The particular system of brisures according to this scheme gained some acceptance in Scotland in the seventeenth century. It was also used to some extent in England. Only a few traces of this system have been found in France.(8)

The mandatory character of differencing in England was brought out in the Court of Chivalry's judgment of 1410 in the case of Grey v. Hastings which is mentioned in Chapter 7. The court held that the heir general was entitled to the undifferenced arms and that the heir male was obliged to bear a differenced version.

The fifteenth century "Ordinances of the Duke of Clarence" required the Kings of Arms to record the names and arms of all nobles and gentlemen as well as "the names of their issue with their true differences".(9)

The necessity for differencing was again brought out in a set of rules which may have been written by Glover, the sixteenth century antiquary. According to this document, all the male line descendants of the first bearer of a particular coat of arms can bear it "with their ordinary differences or extraordinary, as they bear in degrees of kindred to him that first bore it, and to him that is lineally heir to the first bearer of it".(10)

In the seventeenth century Dugdale cited (with apparent approval) Camden's dictum that "when younger brethren do marry, erect, and establish new houses, (they) are accordingly to bear their arms with such distinctions and differences, that they may be known from their elder families". Dugdale also cited other writers of the sixteenth and seventeenth centuries, including Sir Henry Spelman who said that it was not lawful for several persons to bear the same arms, without a due difference, even if they were brothers.(11)

It was felt by at least some Kings of Arms in the seventeenth century that the differencing of arms should not be done informally but should be settled by the heralds. In the passage from Camden which is cited by Dugdale and which is partly quoted above, it is also stated that, with regard to the differences to be borne by the younger brothers who establish "new houses", the King of Arms of the province should be consulted and the differences should be established with his consent, so that he can provide advice and keep a record of the matter. In the instructions given by Clarenceux St. George in 1681 to the heralds who were to conduct Visitations on his behalf, he told them (with regard to "the differences of younger branches") to insert "the known filial distinctions for the immediate younger sons of the eldest house, but for more remote descendants, and for the younger sons of younger sons, you shall respite the assigning such differences to the King of Arms of the Province."(12)

There seems, however, to be little evidence (at least in published material) that much use was made of the opportunities to obtain from the Kings of Arms settlements of permanently differenced arms for the cadet branches of armorial families. Two seventeenth century Letters Patent from the Kings of Arms settling such differences may be instanced. In one, the tincture of the principal charges (two bars) was changed from argent to ermine. In the other, a chief was added to the arms. (In both, the crests were also differenced.)(13)

King James II, during his exile in France after the Revolution of 1688, granted warrants to his herald, Athlone, to examine the pretensions of various persons claiming to be descended from certain English families and, if such descents were established, to grant these persons the arms of the relevant families "with the proper distinctions".(14)

The differencing of arms was considered to be so important a feature of the English law of arms that in addition to stating that the descendants of grantees of arms were to bear them "according to the laws of arms", many English grants of arms have explicitly stated that they were to bear the arms with "due differences". Already common in the sixteenth century, this feature appeared in the majority of grants and confirmations of arms by Letters Patent of the Kings of Arms between the seventeenth and nineteenth centuries.(15)

The Court of Chivalry continued to apply the law regarding differences. An example is found in a decision of the court in the last decade of the seventeenth century. In that case the defendant had been accused of unlawfully bearing arms. The matter was referred to the heralds for their report. A Chapter of the heralds reported that the defendant's father was descended from someone who had been entered at the Visitation of Yorkshire in 1612, and that in consequence the heralds were of opinion that the defendant's father had the right to use the arms in question, but "with a due difference, as being the 4th son of a third house, of a second branch". The Court of Chivalry accordingly monished the defendant to bear the arms with a proper difference.(16)

Notwithstanding all this, the actual practice of differencing fell away sharply in England in the sixteenth century, and by the seventeenth century there were few examples of the practice, apart from some use of the minor cadency marks. Even this use, which was never a general one, soon died out almost completely, although it continued to be described and recommended by writers on heraldry until the twentieth century.(17)

While English grants of arms of the first half of the twentieth century continued for a time to specify that the arms were to be borne by the grantee and his descendants "with due and proper differences according to the laws of arms", the words "with due and proper differences" have been omitted from at least some of the most recent grants. No attempt seems to be made to enforce the differencing of arms (except in the arms of the Royal Family), either by means of the older brisures or by means of minor cadency marks or in any other way. Indeed the English system of differencing according to seniority has recently been described by an English herald as being "permissive rather than mandatory".(18)

It seems, however, that the system is "permissive rather than mandatory" only in that it remains unenforced. That it is "mandatory" in principle is evident from the absence of any known legislative or judicial change in the law. This appears to have been acknowledged by Counsel in the course of a hearing in the Court of Chivalry as recently as 1954; replying to a question from the judge as to whether all the sons of a grantee of arms had the right to bear the arms, Counsel stated that they did "with marks of what is called cadency", and explained that these were additions to the shield to indicate the positions of the sons in the family.(19)

The usual English practice is now (as it has been for a long time) for all legitimate male line descendants of a grantee of arms to use the arms without any difference, although some authors suggest that it is "discourteous" of younger branches not to use some mark of difference from the head of the family.

English women outside the Royal Family do not use differences. As it is the rule that they cannot transmit their father's arms, whole and unquartered, there is generally no point in their differencing these arms, which they can use unaltered.(20)

The practice of differencing in France evolved in a manner not very different from that followed in England. In France as in England it came to be well established law that only the head of a family had full rights in the arms, and that other members of the family were entitled only to differenced versions thereof (although, in France as elsewhere, most women were allowed to use their father's arms undifferenced). The bearer of each differenced version transmitted it to his heir; his other descendants were supposed to introduce further differences. All these points had been established in law by the sixteenth century.(21)

So important was the principle of distinguishing the arms of cadets from those of the head of the family that it was explicitly embodied in certain of the codifications of customary law which were made in various parts of France in the fifteenth and sixteenth centuries.(22)

In those parts of France in which women could transmit arms (as in Champagne) differencing was in principle applicable to their arms. In the absence of sons the eldest daughter was alone entitled to be the holder of the undifferenced arms, and therefore her sisters (if any) were presumably under an obligation to difference their arms from hers.(23)

The law did not specify the system of differencing to be used. It was up to those concerned to select an appropriate method. Guidance could be found in tradition, supplemented by the writings of theorists. Arrangements involving the use of labels, bordures or bastons continued to be advocated and used. Some of the later writers suggested the use of small brisures in the form for example of mullets or annulets, which are reminiscent of the British "minor cadency marks".(24)

As in other non-criminal matters, the enforcing of the law was generally left (at least in the period after the decline of the authority of the heralds) to those whose rights were infringed. The head of the family, as the only "holder" of the undifferenced arms (that is, the person entitled not only to bear but also to transmit the arms), could bring an action before the Royal Courts in order to force other members of the family to difference their arms from his. Similarly, the head of a cadet branch of the family could in principle obtain a court order directing junior members of his branch to difference their arms from his. In response to such actions a head of a branch might adopt a brisure and a cadet of a branch might adopt a further brisure (known in French as a "surbrisure").(25)

One dispute lasted nearly a century, beginning in 1424, when the elder of two brothers of a Norman family attempted to persuade the other to difference his arms. An agreement made between the brothers proved abortive, and twenty-five years later the elder brother began an action in the Bailiwick court. This dragged on, until eventually the sons of the two brothers settled the matter by an agreement made before two notaries in 1522; the cadet gave up the use of the disputed arms but, rather than difference them, he preferred to assume completely new arms.(26)

In 1509 a judgment in an action between two members of the Espagne family ordered one of them not to bear the whole arms undifferenced, since he was descended from a cadet branch.(27)

In 1541 the highest judicial authority, the Royal Council itself, pronounced the final judgment in an action brought by Louis de Pierre-Buffière, head of the family, against François de Pierre-Buffière. The latter was the holder of the principal lands of the family, from which it derived its name. Nevertheless he was ordered, as a cadet, not to bear the undifferenced arms.(28)

In 1636 a revised edition of a collection of legal rules and judgments contained a report of a case heard by the Parlement of Grenoble, the judgement having been given in 1494. This settled a dispute between two branches of the Salvaing family, and ordered the cadet not to bear the undifferenced arms to which only the head of the family was entitled in law. This judgment has been relied on by later writers on both sides of the Channel as illustrating the French rule on differencing. However, it appears that the entire report may be fictitious, having been devised by a member of the Salvaing family who had it inserted in the 1636 book. His purpose was to provide corroboration for a claim that his family had long been an illustrious one (the arms said to have been litigated in 1494 included an alleged "Royal" augmentation). The culprit was a prominent lawyer and student of heraldry, a subject he knew well enough for the alleged judgment (including the rule of law expressed therein) to have the necessary verisimilitude.(29)

Some complaints were made about the widespread neglect of differencing, in the hope that the royal authorities would themselves take steps to enforce the law. For example, during the Estates General of 1614 the representatives of the nobility complained that it was no longer possible to tell, from the arms actually borne, who was the eldest and who was the cadet, or who were the descendants of the main line of a family and who were collaterals. This complaint was mentioned in the preamble to the Edict of 1615, creating the office of Juge d'Armes, and it may have been intended that this officer should help to remedy these abuses.(30)

Nothing effective was in fact done by any royal authority, and it was left to the individual to enforce his rights by a private action in the courts of law. By this time arms were being used more as family cognisances than as means of identifying individuals, and this encouraged a general abandoning of differencing within the family. By the latter part of the seventeenth century it was the usual practice for all members of a family to use the undifferenced arms, although the legal obligation on cadets to use differenced arms continued to be mentioned in books. A Royal Declaration of 1699 confirming certain nobiliary laws in the provinces of Flanders, Hainault and Artois (which had been united to the Kingdom of France during the then King's reign) explicitly confirmed the prohibition on the bearing of undifferenced arms by cadets of noble families.(31)

Scotland is the only country in which the practice of differencing the arms of branches of a family has survived in full vigour. This has been termed "the most striking peculiarity of Scottish heraldry".(32)

Many Scottish grants and matriculations of arms emphasise the requirement of differencing. One older method was to state that the arms concerned were to be borne by the person stated and by his heirs (only); in this way no arms were attributed to descendants other than the heir in each generation, and such other descendants were obliged to obtain arms from the Lord Lyon, who made sure that these arms were differenced versions of the "original" arms. A method commonly used since the mid-nineteenth century is to state that the arms are to be borne by the person stated and his descendants with such "congruent differences" as might subsequently be matriculated for them.(33)

The practical difference between English and Scottish heraldry in modern times does not arise from the content of grants of arms in the two countries since, as we have seen, most modern English grants have recited the need for "due differences". It arises from the fact that the Scottish heraldic authority has, and uses, adequate powers to enforce the law.

The Scottish Act of Parliament of 1592 affirmed the authority of the Lord Lyon to distinguish the arms of cadets with "congruent differences". The Act of 1662 ordered younger brothers to bear arms only with "such distinctions as shall be given by the Lyon King of Arms". The 1662 Act was repealed in 1663, but in 1672 another Act came to reinforce that of 1592. The 1672 Act forbade the use of any arms unless they had been matriculated by the Lord Lyon, who might introduce appropriate differences. Since that time (at least), the Lord Lyon has had all the power he needs to enforce the law, which he does by insisting, when matriculating the arms of a cadet, that they are properly differenced from the arms of the head of the family and from those of other cadets.(34)

As long as he remains a part of the parental household, a younger son of a holder of Scottish arms is permitted to make use, without any formality, of the parental arms with the addition of a "minor cadency mark" of the class described above in connection with English heraldry (a small crescent for a second son, etc.). When a younger son marries and establishes his own household, he is required (if he wishes to use arms) to apply to the Lord Lyon to matriculate a permanently differenced version of the parental arms. This differencing may be effected in various ways, but the most common is to surround the parental arms with one of a wide variety of bordures. The differenced arms which have thus been matriculated are themselves subject to the rules governing Scottish arms; for example they may be transmitted to their holder's own successive heirs while his other descendants must matriculate differenced versions of these differenced arms.(35)

In Scotland as elsewhere, daughters can use their parental arms undifferenced (although of course they cannot transmit them unless they are heiresses). This is considered to be a privilege rather than a disability, and is not insisted on if a daughter living independently desires to use arms which are specific to herself. Thus we find, as early as the sixteenth century, the sister of a Scottish peer bearing a differenced version of her paternal arms. An unmarried daughter who is not the heir to her parental arms can petition the Lord Lyon to matriculate a differenced version of these arms. If she marries and has issue, she can transmit her arms to her heirs, either as their whole arms if they retain her name, or as a quartering if they take her husband's name. (36)

During the lifetime of the holder of any Scottish arms, the heir may use them with a label of three points. This is correct whether the heir is male or female. The use of a label by a female heir is not a modern innovation. Thus Janet Fentoun, daughter and heir-apparent of Walter Fentoun of Blaikie, bore her father's arms with a label in 1448, and dropped the label after his death.(37)

There have been a number of judicial decisions, not only of Lyon Court but also of the Court of Session, which have affirmed and enforced the rule that only one person at a time can be the holder of any Scottish arms, and the concomitant rule that only the heir can be this person. A striking instance is provided by the Dundas case. In 1744 a member of that family matriculated certain arms in Lyon Register. Later the Lord Lyon cancelled this matriculation because he decided that the person who had matriculated the arms was not in fact entitled to those particular arms. The matter was brought before the Court of Session. The interlocutor (judgment) of this court in 1762 in effect confirmed that of the Lord Lyon. The Court of Session found that the arms which had been matriculated were those of the heir of the Dundas family who therefore had "the sole right to use and bear the coat of arms of Dundas of that ilk". The person who had matriculated the arms in 1744 was not the heir; he had obtained the matriculation "by obreption" (deceit) and this gave him no right to use them; the matriculation was to be expunged from the records of the Lord Lyon.(38)

In all three countries there has been one practice which has continued to serve as a form of differencing down to the latest times. This is the marshalling of several arms in one shield. There are many examples in all these countries of the paternal arms being combined, temporarily or permanently, with other arms such as the arms of a wife, of a mother or of another ancestress, or of an office or dignity. When this is done by one member or by one branch of a family, it distinguishes the arms borne by that member or branch from those of other members or branches. This amounts to a form of differencing and may make other differencing unnecessary.(39)

Thus far we have been considering the differencing of arms within what we might call the legitimate natural family. Now we turn to the arms of bastard or adopted children.

In the modern law of all three countries bastards and adopted children have not inherited any armorial rights from their father (that is, the natural father in the case of a bastard, and the adoptive father in the case of an adopted child). Some special or general legislative or prerogative act is required to enable them to bear arms based on their father's arms, and special forms of differencing are used in these arms. (An exception with regard to the first of these two rules is to be found in the case of Scottish bastards.)

In early times a variety of methods was used for differencing the arms of bastards. Some of these methods did not differ from those used for differencing the arms of legitimate cadets. Later it became more common to use bends sinister or their diminutives (bendlets sinister, batons). Later still, national peculiarities developed.(40)

In England, where bastards still do not succeed to their father's arms, a Royal Licence is needed to enable a bastard to bear arms based on his father's but suitably differenced. Batons (sinister) and bordures compony have been used, but since the end of the eighteenth century the usual difference for a bastard is a bordure wavy, except in the case of royal bastards for whom the baton (sinister) is now reserved. If a bastard becomes legitimated by the marriage of his parents in accordance with Acts of Parliament of 1926 and 1959, he still does not inherit his father's dignities, and therefore cannot inherit his father's arms; he can, however, petition for a Royal Licence to enable him to bear a version of his father's arms which includes a difference which need not be a "bastard's" difference. (41)

In Scotland a bastard is treated more favourably than in England in that he is automatically allowed to matriculate a differenced version of his father's arms. In fact, he is treated almost like any other cadet, except that his difference is often identifiable as that of a bastard and that he can never become the heir to the undifferenced arms. A female bastard may similarly matriculate differenced arms (and transmit them to her issue). The mark of bastardy in Scotland (as elsewhere) was often a baton (sinister); it seems that a riband (small bendlet) sable was also used. A bordure compony was often used in later times, especially since the eighteenth century, and is now the standard difference of a Scottish bastard.(42)

It is to be noted that the bordure compony does not always imply bastardy in England, and that the bordure wavy does not denote bastardy in Scotland.(43)

In France, as early as the fifteenth century a bend or bendlet sinister and a baton (sinister couped) were often used as differences in the arms of bastards. It seems that a bordure was also used for this purpose in Burgundy. In 1600 a Royal Edict ordered that bastards should not be automatically entitled to inherit nobility from their fathers; jurists deduced from this that bastards were not entitled to their fathers' arms unless they were legitimated or ennobled. A Royal Law of 1629 (the Code

Michaux) provided that if bastard sons of noble fathers were ennobled by the King, they might bear their father's arms differenced with a bend sinister. In 1697 a Royal Declaration provided that all bastards should have the stigma of bastardy removed on payment of certain fees, and that they should then be free to bear the names and arms of their fathers, provided the arms were distinguished from those of legitimate children by means of "the mark of bastardy". The bend sinister remained the characteristic difference to be used by recognised bastards.(44)

In England an adopted child cannot "inherit" the arms or other dignities of his adoptive father. He may petition for a Royal Licence to enable him to use a differenced version of the arms; the usual difference nowadays is the addition of two linked annulets (two links of a chain) to the shield. If the adopted child is the legitimate natural child of an armigerous man, he may use his natural father's arms.(45)

In Scotland also, an adopted child cannot "inherit" the arms or other dignities of his or her adopted father. Apart from very rare instances of resignation and regrant, there have been modern instances of the Lord Lyon allowing adopted children to matriculate arms similar to those of the adoptive father, but differenced by a voided canton.(46)

In France, adoption remained rare until the Revolution. It has been suggested by a modern writer that an adopted child could assume his adoptive parent's arms. Perhaps this was true only if the adoptive parent was the last of his family, when he might convey his arms to an adopted child, for example by means of a "name and arms" clause in a will or marriage settlement or contract of adoption.(47)

The English officers of arms have been able to continue to enforce differencing of the arms of bastards and adopted children because it is accepted that they do not inherit any armorial rights. The need for a Royal Licence gives the officers of arms the opportunity of specifying precisely the form of the arms they are to receive.

CHAPTER 9

SURVEYS

It appears that in the fifteenth century each of the Kings of Arms in France and England took an oath on appointment which required him to ascertain the "noble gentlemen" or the notable men holding fiefs or other dignities, and to record their names and arms. The oath of the French Kings of Arms is known to have included an undertaking that they would visit the various parts of the kingdom in pursuance of this objective, whenever the King of France issued letters instructing them to this effect. It seems that some such Visitations ("Visites" or "Chevauchées") were in fact carried out in France. There are also traces of some sort of Visitation carried out in Normandy under the authority of the English King towards the middle of the fifteenth century. In England, rudimentary Visitations appear to have taken place at least as early as the second half of the fifteenth century.(1)

In England the practice of making Visitations became well established, and in the course of the sixteenth and seventeenth centuries the Sovereign issued several commissions under the Great Seal directing the two provincial Kings of Arms or their deputies to conduct Visitations in the various counties.

In 1530 King Henry VIII issued Letters Patent for the purpose of assisting Clarenceux in the making of a Visitation wherein he was "to reform all false armory", with power to deface or remove all representations of unwarranted arms. A Visitation commission from Queen Elizabeth in favour of Norroy authorised him to "put down or otherwise deface at his discretion" all arms which were "contrary to the authentic and ancient laws, customs, rules, privileges and orders of arms". Similar duties and powers were specified in a number of later Visitation commissions, until the last such commission was issued shortly before the Revolution of 1688.(2)

Since that Revolution no further Visitations have taken place, although it appears to be still within the powers of the Crown to choose to order further Visitations.(3)

Visitation procedure in the seventeenth century involved the preparation of lists of persons using arms and calling themselves esquires or gentlemen, and summoning such persons to appear before the King of Arms or his deputy to justify their claims to such arms and titles and to record their pedigrees. Persons unable to prove a right to arms might apply for a grant or confirmation of arms. Otherwise they were required to sign a declaration disclaiming any right to arms.(4)

In France the Kings of Arms ceased to make Visitations at an early date, perhaps before the middle of the fifteenth century. A Marshal of Arms appointed by the King of France in 1487 was instructed to make a catalogue of all the arms of the nobles of France, as well as those of Dauphiny and Provence (which had recently been added to the royal dominions), but there seems to be no record of any actual survey.(5)

Thereafter, the only general official survey primarily concerned with arms was the Armorial Général of 1696-1709. As will be seen, this bore very little similarity to the Visitations of the Kings of Arms in France or in England, either in its objectives or in its methods.(6)

An Edict of November 1696 abolished the post of Juge d'Armes and created a number of new bodies ("Maîtrises") which were empowered to register arms presented to them or to give arms to those who requested them. The right to bear arms was defined as belonging to various categories of persons and to all who had any "exemptions, privileges or public rights"; this terminology was so vague as to cover almost anyone. A person who used unregistered arms, or who usurped those of another, would be liable to a fine of 300 livres, and articles bearing the arms were to be confiscated. If a man's arms were registered, his widow could continue to use them; and they would pass by inheritance to his children, provided they were re-registered in the name of the latter within a year of his death. Every registration of arms involved the payment of a fee, which was fixed at 20 livres for an individual person, higher fees being payable for the registration of the arms of corporations, towns, provinces, etc.

The various posts in the "Maîtrises" were intended to be sold. However, there were no takers, and the Royal Council appointed Commissioners to perform their functions, and to authorise an officer called the Keeper of the Armorial Général ("Garde de l'Armorial Général") to deliver certificates of registration. These certificates ("Brevets d'Enregistrement") were stated by the Edict to be equivalent to Letters Patent of arms but not evidence of nobility.

The Keeper of the Armorial Général was Charles d'Hozier, who had been Juge d'Armes until the abolition of this post. The registration procedure, which included the collection of the fees, was farmed out, and offices were opened in all the principal cities of France (but not in the French colonies, where the Edict was not registered and to which it therefore did not apply).

The principal object of the King in creating the Armorial Général was to create a new source of revenue. It was anticipated that many people, especially many non-nobles, would seize the opportunity of obtaining an official recognition of armorial status. However, the public's response to the Edict was disappointing, and soon the Royal Council began to produce Orders intended to encourage or oblige more people to register arms. An Order in Council of January 1697 made it clear that wives or widows who wished to bear their own arms, either alone or accollee with those of their husbands, would have to register them. In March another Order in Council provided that no adult should bear his father's or his mother's arms unless he had had them registered in his own name. Later in the same month the Council ordered a search to be made for those who, instead of registering their arms, had removed them from their coaches, plate, seals and other movables. In December 1697 the Council ordered that lists should be drawn up of persons whose arms were to be registered; persons on these lists were to be obliged to register arms. The

77

Council's intention was to ensure that everyone who could afford it should be provided with arms.

As a result, a large number of persons of modest position found themselves obliged to pay fees for arms they had never used and did not want. This caused an outcry in many places, and eventually, in October 1699, an Order in Council exempted some of the less wealthy sections of society from enforced registration.

Soon the system resting on the Edict of 1696 began to be dismantled. An Edict of August 1700 suppressed the "Maîtrises" (which had never been constituted), and ordered that the descendants of those whose arms had been registered would be entitled to bear these arms without being obliged to re-register them. An Edict of April 1701 re-established the post of Juge d'Armes, to which Charles d'Hozier was reappointed by Letters Patent of 23 August. An Order in Council of 9 March 1706 gave the Juge d'Armes authority to correct, on request, any incorrect arms registered in the Armorial Général.

Registrations of arms in the Armorial Général remained possible until 1709, and then ceased completely.

The zeal of those who applied the Edict of 1696 and the Orders in Council of 1697 resulted in the number of registrations exceeding 100,000. However, many individuals and a number of entire families (including some families of the nobility) managed to escape or avoid the attentions of the officials of the Armorial Général. Those who did not escape but who were recalcitrant, hostile or indifferent to the registration of their arms (among whom were many nobles) often did not trouble to produce their true arms (if they had any). The officials made up arms to be registered in their names. The officials prepared whole series of arms based on a basic model with variants (for example a series of shields party per pale with different tinctures and charged with different charges; or a series of shields charged with different animals) and kept them ready for use. Sometimes more imagination was displayed by the officials, who produced many canting arms, some in rather poor taste.

It has been estimated that only a minority of the arms registered in the Armorial Général had already been borne by the families concerned, and that nearly half were imposed by the officials, often on people who already had different arms. The remainder, forming about 10% of the total, consisted of erroneous variants of old arms.

The registration procedure involved a delay of about three months between the payment of the fees and the delivery of a certificate by the Keeper of the Armorial Général. In order to collect the certificate, it was necessary to present to the relevant official a receipt for the fees. Many of those who had not been able to escape the payment of the fees did not take the trouble to collect their certificates. As a result many of these certificates remained in the hands of the Keeper.

The arms registered in the Armorial Général consisted only of shields of arms. No external ornaments (helms, crests, supporters, etc.,) were registered. It was said at the time that the reason for this was that only permanent armorial features were to be recorded, whereas "the timbres and other ornaments of shields are not at all stable, since they change according to the quality of the persons concerned." As timbred arms could be legally borne only by a minority of those whose arms were registered, the registration of timbres would necessarily have involved the officials in examining evidence as to the status of those whose arms were being registered, whereas all these officials were really intended to do was to expedite the registrations so as to maximise the fiscal efficiency of their operations.(7)

An area in which the officials did have to exercise care was specified in an Order in Council of 19 March 1697. Arms registered were not to include any fleur de lys or on an azure field unless adequate proof was presented to the senior officials in Paris. In consequence, while the local officials did not refuse the fees tendered by persons producing such arms, the arms themselves were often not registered, or the officials simply entered arms of their own devising.(8)

The arms registered in the Armorial Général are blazoned in 34 manuscript volumes, to which correspond 35 volumes in which the arms are depicted. Each province or "Généralité" is represented by one or more volumes of each of these two series. These volumes can be seen in the Bibliothèque Nationale in Paris. The contents of some of them, or parts thereof, have been printed.(9)

It may be worth mentioning that the name "Armorial Général" has been given to various quite different unofficial compilations. The most important of these contains a series of articles on noble families published by two Juges d'Armes in 1738-1768.(10)

Reviewing the provisions of the Edict of 1696 creating the Armorial Général, we find that some of them are reminiscent of the Act of the Scottish Parliament of 1672 creating a register of arms to be kept by the Lord Lyon King of Arms. This applies for example to the obligation of registering all arms which was imposed by both these enactments, and to the penalties they laid down for the use of unregistered arms. However, the systems created by the two enactments turned out in practice to be very different, for not only was the Armorial Général closed after a few years but also it was applied in a manner designed to secure registrations by everyone who could afford the fees.

There is an analogy to be drawn between the Armorial Général and the Visitations of the English Kings of Arms (which had ceased before 1688), in that both were intended to provide a complete register of arms. However, the Armorial Général was drawn up along lines which took no account of whether those registering arms had any pre-existing right to arms, or whether the bearing of arms was appropriate to their style of life.

Half a century after the closing of the Armorial Général there was another royal attempt to create a comprehensive register of all arms in France. The attempt was embodied in an Ordinance which appeared in 1760. This ordered all arms to be registered at a Registry in Paris; those using unregistered arms were to be liable to prosecution. The registration fee ("Droit d'Enregistrement") was fixed at 30 livres for those whose nobility dated from before 1700, as well as for those who had been ennobled since 1700 and had had their arms settled by the Juge d'Armes. Others were also to pay a settlement fee ("Droit de Règlement") of 120 livres. The Ordinance of 1760 differed from the Edict of 1696 in that it restricted the category of those able to bear arms to the nobles and to military officers, officers of the royal households, members of the courts and tribunals, high tax officers, and the magistracy of the towns. Among those excluded were many bourgeois, shopkeepers and artisans who had been obliged to register arms in the days of the Armorial Général! The Ordinance was registered in the secretariat of the Court of the Marshals of France, which was charged with all litigation arising from the Ordinance. The Cour des Aides complained that the Ordinance infringed its established jurisdiction. The Parlement of Paris also intervened and by an "Arrêt" of 22 August 1760 ordered that humble objections should be presented to the King, and that no Ordinance or Declaration relating to armorial matters should be put into effect unless it had been registered by the Parlement. This particular Ordinance was condemned by the Parlement as being contrary to the usages of the Kingdom. The King did not insist, and the Ordinance did not become law.(11)

There was another aspect of the French system which was perhaps more closely analogous than the Armorial Général to the English Visitations. This was the series of Nobiliary Surveys ("Recherches de Noblesse").

The English Visitations were not merely concerned with the recording of arms. In the fifteenth century one of their primary objects was to ascertain the nobles and gentlemen of each armorial province. This remained true of the Visitations until they ceased at the Revolution of 1688, and until then all those who appeared before the Visitation commissioners were required to prove their nobility or gentility. This is exemplified by the particular Visitations mentioned earlier. Thus, the royal Letters

81

Patent of 1530 in favour of Clarenceux stated that he was to conduct a Visitation of his province "by way of nobleness" wherein he was to take note of the pedigrees of those who bore arms. The Visitation commission from Queen Elizabeth in favour of Norroy authorised him to "reprove, control and make infamous by proclamation" anyone who usurped "any name or title of honour or dignity as esquire, gentleman or other", with power in doubtful cases to summon those concerned to appear before the Earl Marshal. Similar language was used in Visitation commissions from Charles II and James II. Those summoned before the heralds on Visitation were required to register their pedigrees and justify their titles of esquire or gentleman as well as their arms. Thus in one of the later Visitations, carried out in 1682, Clarenceux's deputies required the bailiffs of the various hundreds to "warn those baronets, knights, esquires and gentlemen whose names are within written, personally to appear before us"' for the purpose of registering "the descents and arms of all the gentry". In a Visitation made in 1683, a number of persons were warned to appear "for the registering their descents, and justifying their titles of esquire, gentleman, etc" as well as their rights to the arms they bore. In order to prove their right to both arms and gentility those appearing before the Visitation heralds had to produce their pedigrees with suitable proofs. There is little record of the proofs which may have been required in the earlier Visitations. As time went by the heralds became more demanding of documentary evidence or other concrete proofs.(12)

Those found to have usurped gentility might have to sign disclaimers to the titles of esquire and gentleman and to arms, and might have their names published for public obloquy ("made infamous by proclamation"), as being persons who had "usurped the name and title of gentlemen contrary to all right, and to the ancient custom of this land, and the usage of the law of arms". Recalcitrant persons who continued to call themselves gentlemen after being proclaimed no gentlemen in a Visitation could be dealt with by the Court of Chivalry. In 1635 the court ordered a defendant to make public acknowledgement that notwithstanding his having been proclaimed no gentleman during a Visitation in

1623, he had subsequently used "the name and title of gentleman in contempt of the Laws of Arms and of the Court".(13)

The records of the earliest Visitations consist largely of lists of names and arms, and it is not clear how much reliance was placed on proved pedigrees. Soon it became customary to record the pedigrees of those concerned. Initially, pedigrees often consisted of a list of names without dates, perhaps based merely on the asseverations of those concerned. The later Visitations were conducted with greater care in this regard, and by the third decade of the seventeenth century properly drawn up pedigrees based on documentary or other reliable evidence had become common. Much of the material collected by the Visitation heralds between 1530 and 1687 (each county of England was visited at least once, and some were visited several times) has been published.(14)

The French nobiliary surveys seem to have begun as Visitations carried out by the French heralds before the middle of the fifteenth century, in accordance with their oath of creation which required them to ascertain and record the names and arms of the members of the nobility. No Visitations appear to have been carried out after the fifteenth century by the French heralds, whose prestige and powers had become negligible. Nor did their effective successor, the Juge d'Armes, have the resources to undertake any general survey.

However, the principle of such surveys was not abandoned. A main reason was that in many parts of France the possession of nobility implied exemption from the tax known as the "Taille", which became a permanent royal tax in the fifteenth century. In default of officers of arms having the authority and resources necessary for carrying out nobiliary surveys, these were carried out by tax officials or by special commissioners appointed for the purpose.

One of the first of this new series of "Visitations", known as "Recherches de Noblesse", was that of Raymond Monfaut, a high financial official ("Général des Monnaies") who had previously served the English Crown. This survey was carried out in Normandy in 1463-1464. The next survey in that province was carried out in 1523 by the local tax officials known as "Elus". In the first survey, only the names of those found to be noble (and the names of those found to have usurped nobility) seem to have been recorded. In the second, the pedigrees presented were also recorded, as were the arms.(15)

Later similar surveys were carried out in some provinces. For example a Royal Regulation ("Règlement") of 1639 ordered that a search should be carried out in the province of Dauphiny to detect all persons who had usurped nobility since 1599, so that they should not escape paying the "Taille". By this Regulation it was provided that those who could prove peaceable possession of the noble state since at least 1562 were to be accepted as genuinely noble.(16)

In 1655 and 1656 Royal Declarations called for searches to be made for usurpers of nobility (including persons who usurped timbred arms), and further Declarations and Orders in Council followed in 1658, in 1661 and in 1665, but it was not until 1666 that a full search was in fact initiated in most parts of France.(17)

The thorough and extensive survey which began in 1666 was regulated by several Orders in Council. One of these, of March 1666, contained general instructions for the Commissioners who were to carry out the survey in each province. Summonses were to be sent to persons using noble titles requiring them to appear before the Commissioners' officers who would visit the various towns for this purpose. The Commissioners were empowered to issue decisions which were to be final unless appealed to the Royal Council. They were to fine those found to have usurped noble status and those who, having done so, now voluntarily disclaimed any right thereto, the fines in each case being left to the Commissioners' discretion.

When the survey had been completed, a catalogue was to be made of the "names, surnames (i.e., territorial names), arms and domiciles of the true "gentilshommes" to be registered in each Bailiwick".(18)

Those who were summoned to prove their nobility could do so by proving either that they or their ancestors had been ennobled by Letters Patent or by holding an office which conferred nobility on its holders, or that their ancestors had enjoyed noble status since at least 1560.

The survey was pressed forward vigorously for a couple of years, and more slowly until 1674, when it was stopped because of the wars. It was taken up again in 1696, was pursued with decreasing zeal and was finally stopped altogether in 1727. The survey covered most of France, including provinces such as Provence in which the "Taille" was real rather than personal (that is, liability to this tax depended on the status of the land rather than the status of its owner).

The Commissioners who were appointed to carry out the survey in each province were often the Intendants who headed the provincial administration or Masters of Requests. Some were Conseillers (Judges) of one of the "sovereign" courts. None of the officers of arms seem to have been involved, except a Juge d'Armes who was employed to assist the Intendant in the province of Champagne.

A number of exceptions or modifications were applied to the rules governing the conduct of the survey. All officers in the army and navy were exempted from the survey, as were the inhabitants of Navarre and Bearn. In Normandy, it was enough to prove a century of noble status. This last rule was extended to the whole kingdom by Royal Declaration in 1714.(19)

The survey was less perfect in its execution than in its conception. There were mistakes, and no doubt there was some bribery. Some non-noble families were held to be noble, and were consequently incorporated into the nobility, at least as far as the tax collectors were concerned. Some families of the ancient nobility were held to be non-noble; many of those who could afford an appeal to the Royal Council were reinstated in their nobility. A number of families, both of genuine and of doubtful nobility, were able to avoid the survey altogether, and continued to enjoy noble status undisturbed. Nevertheless the results of the survey were sufficiently extensive to provide the basis of a catalogue of the French nobility in the reign of Louis XIV.(20)

Orders in Council of April and June 1683 provided that the decisions of the Commissioners between 1666 and 1674 should be lodged with the Royal Genealogist, together with inventories of the proofs produced, the arms, pedigrees and other documents involved An Order in Council of May 1699 authorised the Royal Genealogist to issue certificates of the decisions of the Commissioners. These provisions were confirmed by another Order in Council in May 1728. The Orders in Council of 1683 and 1728 required the Royal Genealogist to prepare a register of all the families who had been "maintained" noble, but this was never done.(21)

The surviving records of the nobiliary survey begun in 1666 are by no means complete. Many or most of the original documents have been lost, although this loss is partly compensated in some cases by more or less complete or correct copies made at various times. In some provinces only the names of those concerned have been preserved; in others the proved genealogies; in a few, a record of the documents constituting the proofs. In some cases the records have included the names of those who were condemned as usurpers or who voluntarily desisted from claiming noble status. Some of this material has been published.(22)

In Scotland there seem not to have been any general Visitations or other surveys of arms or of nobles which involved sending the officers of arms or other commissioners into all parts of the country.

Although it appears that the ancient oath of creation of the Lord Lyon required him to ascertain the noblemen and gentlemen who should take the field in the King's service, and those who held by knight's fees, yet as far as we know any Visitations which may have been carried out were of restricted scope. An Act of the Scottish Parliament of 1592 gave "full power and commission to Lyon King of Arms and his brother heralds to visit the whole arms of noblemen, barons and gentlemen borne and used within this realm", but this authority seems to have been little used.(23)

An Act of 1672 ordered "all … noblemen, barons and gentlemen who make use of any arms" to produce them to the Lord Lyon with evidence ("testificates") both of the arms being theirs and of their descents to show their position in any armorial family to which they might claim to belong, so that the Lord Lyon might be able to record the arms. The Register in which which the record was made was to be "respected as the true and unrepealable rule of all arms and bearings in Scotland, to remain with the Lyon's Office as a public Register of the Kingdom."(24)

In general it was left to those who had borne arms to present themselves before the Lord Lyon. They were furnished with a strong incentive to do so by the 1672 Act which made the bearing of unrecorded arms unlawful. Moreover there were instances of particular persons being summoned in the King's name to appear before the Lord Lyon, by virtue of Letters of Horning, raised at Lyon's instance, and to produce their arms and justify their descents so that Lyon might distinguish the arms appropriately, and record ("matriculate") them in his Register. Those summoned in this way were punished for using their arms before matriculation thereof by being fined £100 Scots for "the penalty already incurred by you through using your arms".(25)

The fact that the 1672 Act made it unlawful to bear unmatriculated arms has resulted in Lyon's Register (known as the Public Register of all Arms and Bearings in Scotland) being the complete record of all lawfully borne Scottish arms, and this fact has made any other general survey superfluous. The arms in the first Volume of the Register, covering the period from 1672 to 1804, have been published, and there is a published Ordinary covering the period from 1672 to 1973.(26)

The Lord Lyon will adjudicate on pedigrees presented to him. Approved pedigrees may be recorded in a Public Register of Genealogies which has been maintained by the Lord Lyon since at least the seventeenth century. Moreover, the Lord Lyon has been granting certificates of descent or certified pedigrees ("Birthbriefs") since at least the sixteenth century. These give the arms of the person concerned, and often also give those of the families from which he descends in various lines. Such birthbriefs sometimes state explicitly that the person concerned is of noble or gentle descent. They have been received abroad as evidence of nobility, enabling persons of Scottish descent naturalised in foreign countries to be officially received into the nobility of such countries.(27)

In England, while there has been no general survey of arms or pedigrees since the Revolution of 1688, use has been made of a procedure which has existed since the sixteenth century whereby the officers of arms certify arms and pedigrees which have been presented to and verified by them, or which have been traced by them. Pedigrees approved by them may be recorded in the College of Arms. Pedigrees certified by the Kings of Arms demonstrating that a person is descended of a line of gentlemen bearing arms have been accepted abroad as evidence that the person concerned is fit to be received officially into the local nobility. Moreover, a number of Letters Patent of arms issued by the English Kings of Arms in the sixteenth and seventeenth centuries contained a more or less detailed account of the ancestry of the beneficiaries, sometimes stating explicitly that they were of ancient and noble lineage.(28)

In France, the cessation of work on the nobiliary survey by 1727 was followed by a Royal Declaration of 1729 which ordered that any pending matter should be decided by the relevant Cour des Aides.

All future decisions on nobiliary status which might be required for fiscal purposes (the nobles were exempted from the "Taille" in some parts of France) were to be made by the Cour des Aides. The Declaration expressly preserved the competence of the

Parlements and the inferior courts (Bailiwicks and Seneschalcies) to hear cases in which questions of nobility were involved.(29)

A number of places at Court and elsewhere were restricted to persons whose ancestors had been noble for several generations. The hereditary nature of arms made it necessary for the Juge d'Armes to be expert in genealogy, and it was natural that he should be selected by the King to verify the nobiliary qualifications of candidates for such places. Among the first places to be affected were those of the Pages of the Royal Stables (boys who attended the King and were educated at his expense). In 1643 the King ordered that his Pages must prove that their families had been noble for at least four generations, and he entrusted the verification of the proofs to the Juge d'Armes.

Later the Juge d'Armes was given analogous functions in connection with candidates for the Royal School for Young Ladies at St. Cyr (founded in 1686) and for the Royal Military School (founded in 1751). The Juge d'Armes was sometimes approached directly by persons who wanted him to verify their pedigrees for private purposes, or for possible future use. The various certified pedigrees emanating from the Juge d'Armes included the arms of the family concerned, and in some cases the arms of marriage alliances.(30)

Some verifications of nobility were in the province of the Royal Genealogist rather than the Juge d'Armes. After the introduction (in 1781) of a rule which restricted commissions in certain regiments to those who had at least four generations of nobility, it was the Royal Genealogist who was charged with checking their proofs. He had already had much experience of this sort of thing. When someone applied to the Royal Council for an Order confirming his nobility (either to quash an unfavourable finding by the Commissioners carrying out the Survey of 1666 etc., or for any other reason), the Royal Genealogist was usually asked to consider the matter and to prepare a report for the assistance of the Council. If a noble residing in the French West Indies wished to make use of his titles (for example the "basic" noble title of "Ecuyer") he was first obliged by law to register his nobility at the local Conseil Supérieur; after 1745, such registration involved obtaining the permission of the Minister of the Navy and Colonies, who referred the matter to the Royal Genealogist.

It was also the Royal Genealogist who advised the King about the antiquity of the nobility of persons who desired to receive Court Honours ("Honneurs de la Cour"). These honours consisted (for men) in being allowed to get into one of the King's carriages and follow him when he went hunting or (for women) in being presented at Court. The King could of course admit or reject anyone he chose, but as a general guide he laid down in 1759 and 1760 that persons who wished to enjoy Court Honours should be in possession of nobility dating from before 1400; exceptions might be made for the families of Marshals of France, of Chevaliers of the Holy Ghost and of the King's Ministers. Court Honours were eagerly sought by those who thought they might be admitted to them, and for this purpose a number of provincial nobles made the journey to Versailles once in their lives, returning home to bask in the reflected glory of the Court.(31)

CHAPTER 10

HUSBAND AND WIFE

The unity created by marriage is reflected to a greater or lesser extent in the rules relating to the bearing of arms by each of the spouses.

When two people marry, each may have his or her own arms, or neither may have any arms, or one may have arms but not the other. We will consider the three situations in which at least one has arms; these situations are, firstly, that in which the groom has arms but the bride has none (that is, she is neither a holder of arms nor the daughter of a holder of arms); secondly, that in which the bride has arms but the groom has none; and thirdly, that in which both groom and bride have arms.

If the groom has arms and the bride has none, then both members of the married pair can use the groom's arms. This is a universal principle in the heraldry of all three countries.(1)

If the bride has arms and the groom has none, the rules vary from country to country. We will first consider the wife, and then the husband.

In Scotland the position of the wife has been made clear, and it is a favourable one as compared with other countries. She may simply continue to use her arms after marriage as she did before marriage, depicted on a lozenge or oval shield.(2)

In France, a wife who was of an armigerous but non-noble family (that is, a family able to bear un-timbred arms only) could continue to use these arms after marrying a non-armigerous man. If the wife was of a noble family, she lost her nobility when she married a non-armigerous man as he was necessarily non-noble, and presumably she could in law no longer use her family's noble arms. (The situation was no doubt different in those areas of the country where nobility could be retained and even transmitted by

91

a noble woman married to a non-noble man.) The present paragraph is based on general principles and on the opinions of some commentators; it does not seem to be supported by any judicial decision or official statement.(3)

In England, a resolution of a Chapter of Heralds in 1562, which appeared to forbid the use of arms by any woman married to "any that is no gentleman", has been taken as making it impossible for a married woman to use her arms except when combined with her husband's arms. Consequently, if the husband has no arms, it has been the practical rule that the wife is unable to use arms. In more recent times there has been an indication that the matter may be reconsidered.(4)

Turning now to consider the position of a nonarmigerous groom who marries a bride who bears arms, we may begin by noting that in medieval times there were many examples of an "incoming" husband taking the arms, and often also the name, of his wife, especially when she was an heiress.

This custom has been embodied in the law of Scotland to this extent, that the husband of a female holder of arms (by which we mean, as explained in Chapter 7 , a woman entitled both to bear and transmit the arms) may himself bear her arms "by the courtesy of Scotland", provided he also takes her name. If the arms have been matriculated in his wife's name they need not be re-matriculated for him, but his taking of her name should be signified to the Lord Lyon. The husband's right to bear the arms is essentially dependent on his marriage to the holder, so that, although he can continue to use them after her death, they can be transmitted only to her children and not to any children he might have of another wife (he is, in other words, in much the same position as a wife who bears her husband's arms).(5)

In England where, as we have seen, an armigerous woman loses the ability to use her arms if she marries a man who has no arms of his own, the man himself does not acquire any rights in her arms.

However, the position can be saved if she is an heiress by petitioning for a Royal Licence to enable the husband to bear his wife's name and arms. The destination (limitation) specified in the Royal Licence or in the subsequent Letters Patent of the Kings of Arms may indicate whether the husband can transmit the arms even to children which he may have by another marriage.(6)

In France it remained relatively easy for a man to adopt his wife's arms, and even her name, provided he did not infringe the rights of someone else. If she was the last of her name it was very unlikely that anyone else would have any rights which might be infringed by a husband who adopted her arms. Many marriage contracts and wills which required the taking of a wife's arms as a condition for succeeding to property were given effect by the authorities; in some cases specific royal approval for the armorial transfer was obtained, in others no such approval was deemed necessary. One of the last instances was in 1780, when the Juge d'Armes gave his approval to a newly ennobled man taking the arms of his wife who was the sole heiress of her family. In such cases the husband could acquire full rights in the arms; if his wife died and he had children from a later marriage, these children could inherit the arms.(7)

If both groom and bride have arms, various alternatives may be open to them. One alternative, equally available in England, France and Scotland, is for both spouses to bear the husband's arms alone, those of the wife being ignored.(8)

Another alternative is for each spouse to continue to bear the arms he or she bore before the marriage. This is possible in Scotland. It is not possible in England since, as already indicated, it is held there that a married woman can use her maiden arms only in combination with those of her husband. This alternative was possible in France, at least if both spouses were noble. It is true that the English view had some adherents; thus, in 1504 a French lawyer was of the opinion that a condition in a will requiring the bearing of certain arms would be impertinent if applied to women "as they cannot bear arms, since they take their honour and arms from their husband". However, this could not have been said in those parts of France (such as Champagne) in which noble women could transmit both nobility and arms to their issue even when their husbands were not noble. Moreover, many married women had their paternal arms (alone) registered in their names in the Armorial Général of 1696-1709.(9)

A third alternative is for both arms to be combined, the combined arms being borne by both spouses (or sometimes, if preferred, by the wife alone; the husband then bears only his own arms).(10)

There are at least four ways in which the combination may be made. One is to impale the arms of both spouses in one shield. Another is to use two shields accollee. In both these cases it is the husband's arms which are placed on the dexter side. A third way is to quarter the arms, the principal quarters being usually occupied by the husband's arms. A fourth way is to place the wife's arms on a small shield over the centre of the husband's shield (as with the so-called "inescutcheon of pretence"). Custom and usage have resulted in some definition of the circumstances in which each of these ways may be followed.

In England the normal practice is to impale both arms in one shield. If the wife is an heiress, it is more usual to use an "inescutcheon of pretence", although the impaled shield may be used if preferred. It was believed at one time that a husband could not use the inescutcheon of his heiress wife unless and until a child had been born of the marriage. This rule was propounded by the King's Advocate in a case before the Court of Chivalry at the beginning of the eighteenth century. The defendant, who had married an heiress but had not had a child by her, denied that there was such a rule. No decision is recorded. Accollee shields are not generally used in England, except when there is a special reason for their use (the most common such reason is a desire to include arms of office, with which we are not concerned). Quartered shields of the arms of husband and wife were sometimes used in medieval England, but this practice seems to have ceased before 1500, and has been considered incorrect since the sixteenth century.(11)

In Scotland the normal practice is to impale both arms in one shield. This is so even if the wife is an heiress; the "inescutcheon of pretence" is not favoured by the Lord Lyon, as not being in accordance with ancient Scottish practice, although it is sometimes used, especially if the wife is a peeress in her own right in which case the inescutcheon may be ensigned with her coronet as is done in England. Accollee shields may be used if desired; they may have to be used for special reasons (as in England). Quartered shields of the arms of husband and wife were sometimes used in Scotland, especially if the wife was an heiress. This practice seems to have existed in the eighteenth century. Even today, it remains possible in certain circumstances. If the wife is an heiress whose name is not to be retained by the issue of the marriage then, after the couple have had at least one child, the husband may apply to the Lord Lyon to matriculate arms in which his and his wife's arms are quartered; the arms thus matriculated will descend to the heir of the marriage.(12)

In France it was the general practice since the seventeenth century for combination of the arms of spouses to be effected by means either of an impaled shield or of accollee shields. It was not uncommon, at least until the sixteenth century, for such a combination to be effected by quartering, and there were many examples (especially when the wife was the last of her family, or of a branch thereof) of a husband or a wife, or both, using a quarterly shield in which the husband's arms were (usually) placed in the principal quarters and the wife's arms in the remaining quarters. It was not normal French practice to use an inescutcheon of a wife's arms on a shield of her husband's arms.(13)

CHAPTER 11

TIMBRES AND ACCESSORIES

While the so-called rules relating to the form, disposition and tinctures of heraldic charges on shields are only conventions, some at least of the rules relating to the external ornaments or accessories of the shield have a legal sanction.

In French heraldry the most important accessory was the timbre, by which was meant a helm (or sometimes a coronet).(1)

The importance of the timbre lay in that it was, in law, a sign that the bearer was noble.(2)

While the French monarch felt unwilling or unable to accede to requests from the nobles that non-nobles should be forbidden to bear any arms at all, he did legislate to declare it illegal for them to bear timbred arms. An early general enactment to this effect was an Ordinance of 1560 which provided that those who usurped nobility and bore timbred arms were to be fined by the judges.

These provisions were confirmed by an Edict of 1579, and by further Edicts or Declarations of 1583, 1634 and 1656. In 1661 the King ordered that the timbres placed over the shields of arms of persons who had usurped nobility and timbred arms should be defaced and broken, and such persons should be fined. In Provence these provisions were reinforced by a Royal Declaration in 1665. A few years after the province of Franche-Comté had been united to the Kingdom of France, a Declaration of 1699 concerned with the affairs of that province contained a confirmation of the prohibition on the bearing of timbred arms by non-nobles.(3)

Ennoblement conferred the right to place a timbre over the arms of the ennobled person. Three Edicts which provided for the ennoblement of large numbers of persons (50 in 1645, 500 in

1696 and 200 in 1702) contained specific references to the right of these new nobles to bear timbred arms. Letters Patent of ennoblement granted by the King to individuals might state explicitly that the ennobled person was permitted to bear timbred arms.(4)

The law was enforced by the courts in the sixteenth and seventeenth centuries. As early as 1556 a judgment of the Parlement of Paris ordered the breaking of the timbred arms borne by someone whose claim to nobility was false. In 1607 a judgment of the Parlement of Dijon imposed a fine of 500 livres on a non-noble who had timbred his arms on a monument in a church, and called the attention of the public to the prohibition of the use of timbred arms by non-nobles. The next year the same court imposed a fine of 1000 livres on the heirs of a man whose arms had appeared with a timbre in a church; he had purchased the lands of a barony but this in itself did not make him noble. The same court enforced the law again in judgements of 1625 and 1655. In the latter case, a non-noble advocate or barrister who had placed on his wife's tomb a representation of her arms timbred with a cordeliere was ordered to deface the arms and to pay a fine of 500 livres. The judgement included another warning to the public against usurping the titles of "Noble" and "Ecuyer", and against usurping timbred arms. The Parlement of Paris also continued to enforce the law; in 1663 it issued an order ("Arrêt en forme de Règlement") which again forbade the bearing of timbred arms by non-nobles.(5)

The other "sovereign" courts also applied the law on timbred arms when dealing with cases within their jurisdiction. Between 1662 and 1665 the Cour des Aides of Paris pronounced judgement in several hundred cases in which persons who bore timbred arms were accused of usurping the noble state. Those found guilty were fined 2000 livres, and the timbre attached to their arms was ordered to be defaced.(6)

So strong was the legal connection between nobility and timbred arms, that it was believed that if the King made a grant of timbred arms (without any explicit reference to nobility) to a person who in fact was not already noble, such a grant amounted to an ennoblement. Thus the Commissioners who carried out the great Nobiliary Survey of 1666 in Provence accepted that a particular family was noble because its founder had been granted timbred arms by the King in 1524.(7)

There was thought to be an exception to the law forbidding the bearing of timbred arms by non-nobles. In 1371 Royal Letters Patent were issued which granted or confirmed certain privileges to be held by the burgesses of Paris. From the sixteenth century onwards it was understood that one of these privileges was that of bearing timbred arms. This was really a misunderstanding of the Letters Patent of 1371, which had said nothing about timbred arms, but the royal authority appears to have accepted the new interpretation put on the Letters Patent, which accordingly became an effective rule.(8)

In the eighteenth century the Juge d'Armes was able not only to settle the arms of those newly ennobled by the King (as he had already done in the seventeenth century) but also to settle both timbred and untimbred arms for qualified persons who approached him for this purpose so as to obtain official evidence of their arms. As has been mentioned in Chapter 5, the settlements of arms issued by the Juge d'Armes were not in law the same as grants of arms, which were reserved to the King himself. It was, strictly speaking, beyond the power of the Juge d'Armes to settle timbred arms for someone who was not already noble. On the whole the Juge d' Armes appears to have observed this rule; his settlements in favour of priests, non-noble civil servants, judges and other officers of the lower courts (Bailiwicks and Seneschalcies), military officers of low rank, and burgesses of towns other than Paris did not include timbres; also refused timbres were non-noble holders of fiefs. Most of those whose settlements included timbres were already in full possession of nobility, either inherited or recently acquired. Burgesses of Paris were allowed timbres, for the reason mentioned above. The Juge d'Armes did not refuse timbres for persons who held civil or military posts which conferred nobility automatically if held for a certain period of years or for two or three generations. Some persons holding posts which entitled them to a purely personal title of "Noble" or "Ecuyer" which they could not transmit to their posterity were also allowed timbres. There may have been instances of even greater laxity.(9)

The King's intention that the law should not be changed is demonstrated by the abortive Ordinance of 1760 mentioned in Chapter 9. This provided that the fine for any non-noble (other than a burgess of Paris) who placed a timbre over his shield was to be 3000 livres. Until the Revolution the illegality of the use of timbred arms by non-nobles other than these burgesses continued to be mentioned in legal treatises.(10)

There seems never to have existed in England any rule which forbade the bearing of a helm by any man who was entitled to bear a shield of arms. Nor has there been any such rule in Scotland, at least since the seventeenth century. Any man in England or Scotland who is entitled to bear a shield of arms is also entitled to timbre his shield. Such rules as exist relate only to the detailed form of the timbre.(11)

Until the sixteenth century those who chose to place helms over their shield, whether in France or in Britain, selected whatever shape pleased them. Some form of closed helm was generally used, and most helms were placed in profile over the shield. Later the heralds or their voluntary advisers developed a number of schemes in which different helms were assigned to different ranks, titles or degrees.(12)

It seems that it was only in the seventeenth century that the barred helm came into general use by peers in England and Scotland, and that the open, full-fronted helm became distinctive of knights (and baronets). This left untitled gentlemen in possession of the older forms of helm. From this situation was developed the modern "hierarchy" of three or four helms in English heraldry, and up to six in Scottish heraldry. This arrangement has been given some official sanction by the Kings of Arms.(13)

A somewhat analogous but rather more uncertain evolution occurred in French heraldry. By the early part of the seventeenth century writers on heraldry were formulating "rules", which generally assigned a closed helm placed in profile to an ennobled person, and barred helms to those who were noble by birth or who held certain titles or military commands. More specific details were the subject of a great diversity of opinion. Helms were often classified according to the number of bars or grills from, say, three for a "simple" noble to, say, seven or even eleven for a marquis, but in practice little attention was paid to such classifications, which seem never to have received any official sanction, and people generally used whatever number of bars they happened to like.(14)

Some guidance as to the "official" view may be derived from the settlements of timbred arms made in the eighteenth century by the Juge d'Armes. The timbre was usually a helm, which generally had one of three positions. If the person concerned was newly ennobled, or possessed personal but not hereditary nobility, or was a burgess of Paris, the helm was usually closed and in profile. Sons of ennobled persons had a (barred) helm turned at an angle ("taré de deux tiers"), and from the fourth generation of nobility it was permissible to turn it somewhat more towards the front ("taré de trois quarts"). However, exceptions were not uncommon.(15)

In the seventeenth century a French heraldic writer, moved by the plight of some military officers who were not noble and were therefore not entitled to use a helm, suggested that they might ensign their shields with a gorget through which passed a pikestaff placed vertically behind the shield. This proposal does not seem to have been widely followed, and it received no official sanction.(16)

French helms, like British helms, might be surmounted by a wreath (whether or not a crest was placed thereon), and might be equipped with a mantling, The customs relating to these accessories and their tinctures did not differ significantly. In grants and settlements of arms there might be specific definitions of the tinctures. Thus it seems that in settlements of timbred arms made by the Juge d'Armes in the eighteenth century, the helm was always accompanied by a mantling having the tinctures of the field and the principal charges of the shield. This was in conformity with widespread practice, not only in France, but also in Britain (although there was a time when British mantlings tended to be gules lined argent or (for peers) ermine; such mantlings are still used systematically for certain categories of Scottish peers).(17)

In medieval times some Kings and great nobles placed coronets above their shields. Sometimes their crests were supported by coronets. In the sixteenth century it became common for the higher nobles to use coronets of various patterns.(18)

In Britain the use of coronets came to be controlled by the heralds, basing themselves on royal commands as to the particular coronets which were to be worn by the peers on certain occasions. The different ranks of the peerage were provided with different coronets. The lowest rank was the last to be assigned its coronet. In 1660 Charles II assigned a coronet to the Barons of England, and in 1665 he granted another Royal Warrant to be recorded by the Lord Lyon, which permitted the same coronet to be used by the Scottish Lords.(19)

In British heraldry, peerage coronets are important. They correspond to specific titles which all have considerable significance (for example in relation to the Upper House of Parliament), and there is a clear gradation of rank and precedence between the different titles. In French heraldry coronets were much less important. The "titles" they represented (except that of duke) were mere decorations to which were attached no special privileges or precedence. This was no doubt why, apart from the basic laws which forbade all timbres to non-nobles, there were few officially sanctioned rules relating to coronets.

In 1663 the Parlement of Paris ordered that only those who had been created baron, count or marquis by Letters Patent should use such titles and bear their coronets over their arms. In 1699 a

Royal Declaration confirming certain local laws in Artois and in parts of Flanders and Hainault specified that those who usurped full-faced helms or the coronets of princes, dukes, marquises and counts were liable to be fined 300 florins.(20)

The particular forms of coronet were not laid down by law but, as in the case of the helm, the heraldic writers were eager to propose a variety of patterns. It became conventional to distinguish various patterns as being, one that of a count, another that of a baron, and so on, but in practice those who used coronets over their shields selected whatever pattern they pleased.

It may be of interest to compare the conventionally named French coronets with the more precisely-defined British coronets. The basic pattern of the ducal coronet is much the same in the two systems; from a gold circlet rise eight fleurons or "strawberry leaves", five of which are visible in representations. The coronets of British viscounts, earls and marquesses differ only in degree from the French coronets bearing corresponding names. The French baron's coronet or "tortil" is very distinctive; it consists of a circlet around which is wound a string of pearls. British peerage coronets are usually lined with a red velvet bonnet with ermine edging and a golden tassel. French coronets are usually represented without such a bonnet, and this creates an immediate visual distinction between the two sets of coronets.(21)

In English and Scottish heraldry a distinction has long been made between peerage coronets (which are never used to support a crest) and "crest coronets" which are sometimes used in place of (or even in addition to) a wreath for the purpose of supporting a crest. These latter coronets are not restricted to peers. They were at one time relatively freely allowed by the Kings of Arms. It seems that nowadays the English Kings of Arms no longer include them in grants, but the descendants of those to whom they may have been granted continue to use them. Nowadays too, the Lord Lyon allows such coronets sparingly, for example in grants or rematriculations of the arms of chiefs of considerable families.(22)

In French heraldry any type of coronet might be used in any way. Anyone who used a coronet could use it to support his crest (if he had one). If he used a coronet and a helm in the same achievement, he might follow the common British custom of placing the helm and crest above a peerage coronet. Alternatively, he might place the crest on the coronet and the coronet on the helm; this resembled the British practice when the coronet is only a "crest coronet" and not a peerage coronet. It was, however, not common in later French heraldry to use both a helm and a coronet; most representations of arms contained one or the other. In the seventeenth century the helm was more common, but in the eighteenth century the use of coronets became widespread.

In addition to the various helms and coronets, each heraldic system had certain peculiar forms of headgear which are occasionally met in practice. In England there is the cap of maintenance, or chapeau, which Edmondson says was used by Barons before they were allowed a coronet by Charles II; it was later granted to certain ordinary gentlemen, but since the nineteenth century it has been granted to peers only. The chapeau is nowadays particularly allowed in Scotland to "feudal barons" who may not be peers.(23)

One form of headgear which was peculiar to French heraldry was the "mortier", which was a low crowned generally cylindrical bonnet worn by judges of the "sovereign" courts. It is sometimes found ensigning French shields of the seventeenth or eighteenth century; its use in this way was generally restricted to the Presidents of the Parlements. Sometimes it was placed on a full-faced helmet. At other times it was placed inside a coronet.(24)

Notwithstanding the efforts of the authorities to emphasise and enforce it, the French law forbidding the bearing of timbred arms by non-nobles came to be widely flouted. Already in the seventeenth century there were a number of bourgeois who "decorated" their shields with helms. Some, as we have seen, were prosecuted. Nevertheless, their number grew in the eighteenth century, to such an extent that representations of timbred arms could no longer be taken as indicating even a probability that the bearer was noble. As for coronets, they were widely taken, and not only by nobles with any title, or with no title beyond the basic one of "ecuyer" or "chevalier"; the better off members of the bourgeoisie seem to have been particularly fond of the coronet of a "count" although some, like Voltaire, preferred that of a "marquis".(25)

The authorities did not always behave consistently. The Juge d'Armes was sometimes lax in including helms when settling the arms of persons who did not have full hereditary nobility. The King himself might grant exemptions from the law. In 1768, by the King's special permission, the Juge d'Armes included a helm in his settlement of the arms of a merchant of Rouen. At least the Juge d'Armes does not seem to have included unjustified coronets in his settlements; indeed, his settlements of even nobles' arms did not normally include coronets unless the King's specific approval had been obtained, and this was rare.(26)

While the timbre of seventeenth and eighteenth century French heraldry was a helm, or sometimes a coronet, this word had originally meant a crest. Indeed, it is possible that the earliest of the legal prohibitions on the use of a timbre by non-nobles was directed against the use of a crest. In medieval heraldry the use of crests seems to have been associated with tournaments, which were a pursuit of some of the richer or more powerful personages of the realm, and it seems that crests were not much used by the less important bearers of arms. After the heyday of the tournament had passed, the use of crests tended either to die out or, on on the contrary, to become disseminated among almost all holders of arms. The first path was followed in France, the second in England and to a large extent in Scotland; both paths led to crests no longer being the mark of any particular status.

Since the sixteenth century the English Kings of Arms have been granting crests to anyone who requests them, either as part of a grant of arms or as an addition to an existing shield of arms.(27)

In Scotland, it seems that it was only after 1672 that crests were granted by the Lord Lyon to anyone who applied for them; before that date ordinary Scots gentlemen are said to have been allowed shields only, which presumably implies that they had no crests.(28)

In France, the use of crests seems to have almost died out by the middle of the seventeenth century, leaving the name timbre to be applied to what still remained above the shield - the helm. A few people continued to use crests, now called "cimiers", and there was a modest revival of their use in the eighteenth century, but the proportion of armigers who used them remained small. There were no real regulations governing their use, and they were taken, modified or abandoned at will. By special request, crests were included in some of the settlements of arms issued by the Juge d'Armes in the eighteenth century (29)

We have thus far been concerned with methods of ensigning the shield of a man. When the same shield is used by his wife, she may retain all his accessories, although for her personal use she may prefer to omit his helm and crest. Any arms which a woman bears otherwise than in right of her husband (for example arms granted to her or inherited by her) may be subject to certain conventions or rules.

In medieval times some women displayed their arms on shields timbred with a helm and sometimes with a crest. However, it became accepted in France that this was improper as military ensigns were unsuitable for women. The same thing happened in England, where a formal resolution of the heralds in the early years of Elizabeth's reign declared that no woman could bear a crest; the only exception is a reigning Queen.(30)

In Scotland the position is different. The majority of ladies who matriculated arms before 1820 were allowed crests. In the nineteenth century English views were adopted by at least some Scottish writers and heralds, and it was suggested that grants or matriculations of crests in the names of ladies were effective only for their male heirs. In the twentieth century the old Scots law and practice have been affirmed in Lyon Court. While helms are no longer allowed to ladies, and while most ladies do not have a crest, a lady who is the head of her family may place over her lozenge the crest associated with the arms of the head of the family, and a grant of arms to a woman may include a crest for her own use in this way.(31)

A feature of Scottish heraldry found neither in France nor in England is that all members of a family, male and female, can make use of a badge consisting of the crest of the head of the family surrounded by a strap and buckle on which appears the motto of the head of the family.(32)

A lady may ensign her arms with a coronet, being either the coronet of her husband or that of any dignity which she personally holds. This convention applies to the heraldry of all three countries.(33)

Apart from the timbre, the only accessory which had any legal sanction in France was the "cordeliere" or knotted cord used by some women to surround their shields or lozenges. It may have originated in France. It seems to have been more particularly associated with widows, although it was sometimes used by others. It seems to have been regarded at one time and in some provinces as a form of timbre, and therefore forbidden for use by women who were not noble. In 1655 the Parlement of Dijon ordered the defacement of certain arms surrounded by a cordeliere which a lawyer had placed on the tomb of his wife; in its judgment the court referred to the prohibition on the bearing of timbred arms by non-nobles. It may be that the court was influenced by the law in the neighbouring province of Franche-Comté, which was still a part of the Spanish dominions. In 1650 an Edict of Philip IV laid down that only the wives of chevaliers were entitled to use a cordeliere; this Edict was confirmed in 1699 after Franche-Comté had become part of the Kingdom of France. The use of the cordeliere was introduced into Britain, and it is sometimes found surrounding the arms of widows in England and in Scotland.(34)

Mottos and supporters remained unregulated in France, but became subject to rules in Britain. Frenchmen were free to adopt, discard or alter their mottos, or to abstain from the use of one.

In some families long continued use of a particular motto might lead to that motto becoming more closely associated with that family than with others. Some settlements of arms issued in the eighteenth century by the Juge d'Armes included a motto. No distinction was made between nobles and non-nobles. A motto might be depicted either above the timbre or below the shield; some said that the first of these positions was more appropriate for a war-cry ("cri") and the second for a motto proper ("devise"), but there was no consistency of usage.(35)

In England, mottos are rarely specified in grants of arms although, if desired by the grantee, they may be shown in the representation of the arms in the margin of the Letters Patent. They are usually placed below the shield. The use of mottos is free: they may be changed at will. However, it is traditional for English women not to use mottos, although mottos have been shown in some modern grants to women.(36)

In Scotland, mottos (formerly known as "dittons", from the French "dicton" which means a saying) are included in grants and matriculations of arms, which specify their position (usually above the crest). They cannot be changed without a rematriculation. Those women who are entitled to use crests are also entitled to use mottos.(37)

Supporters were an optional and variable feature of armorial achievements in all countries until at least the sixteenth century. In England there were a number of ordinary gentlemen who still used supporters in the seventeenth century, but by that time the heraldic executive was generally applying a rule that supporters were a prerogative of peers, to whom were soon added some other favoured persons, including Knights of the Garter and Knights Grand Cross of certain orders. Specific grants of supporters were made to those who were qualified. It seems that in 1672 Charles II sought to extend the English rule to Scotland by writing to the Lord Lyon that supporters should not be granted to persons who were not peers, but no formal Warrant was issued to this effect, and Lyon soon resumed the practice of granting supporters to certain other armigers, in accordance with older Scottish practice. By the early nineteenth century supporters were being granted to practically anyone who asked Lyon for them. However, later Lyons regarded this as being tantamount to an abuse, and although they have retained a discretion in the matter, this discretion is carefully exercised, although less restrictively than would result from applying the English rule. In England and in Scotland, supporters are transmitted to only one person at a time; in England this is normally the heir male while in Scotland it may be the heir of line, male or female (unless a restriction is expressed in the grant).(38)

In France the situation was different. Supporters never ceased to be a decorative option. Anyone was free to use them, although they became less unusual in the course of the eighteenth century. If requested, the Juge d'Armes was prepared to include supporters in his settlements of arms; in this respect no distinction seems to have been made between nobles and non-nobles.(39)

As a postcript to this chapter, a word will be said about the shape of the shield itself.

The shape of a man's shield has varied in accordance with fashion. In France, the more or less triangular shield frequently used everywhere in medieval times had given way, by the seven-teenth century, to an almost square shield with rounded lower corners and a small point protruding from the base. Although somewhat similar shields are sometimes found in Britain, this shield was so generally used in France that it may be considered a characteristically French shield. It was, however, subject to a decrease in popularity in the eighteenth century, when various neo-classical and rococo cartouches were widely used in accordance with the prevailing tastes in decorative arts.(40)

There has been a tendancy for women's shields to be given "non-military" shapes. Some English women used lozenge-shaped shields as early as the thirteenth century (lozenges were also used by some men until a somewhat later period). In 1562 the English heralds resolved that the arms of unmarried women must be displayed on lozenges. Ordinary shields continued to be used by many ladies in Scotland until a later date; so late as 1880 the Lord Lyon allotted an ordinary shield to a lady. Lozenges were also widely adopted by French ladies.

Indeed, by the seventeenth century it was common practice in all three countries for the arms of women, especially unmarried women and widows, to be displayed on lozenges, although married women often continued to use ordinary shields. Oval shields for women came into fashion in France in the seventeenth and eighteenth centuries, and more recently this fashion has been adopted to some extent in Britain.(41)

CHAPTER 12

"TOKENS OF NOBLENESS"

At several places we have referred to arms and simultaneously to nobility or gentility. Was there a connection between these things? If there was a connection, was it a necessary one? Are arms like names, which can be used to identify nobles and gentlemen but which can also be used by others? Or is their use restricted to the former?

Before examining what can be deduced in this respect from judgements of the courts, from statutes or from other authoritative sources, we will describe, briefly and somewhat superficially, what is or was meant in each of the three countries by terms such as nobility and gentility.

The term "nobility" or "noblesse" had recognisably similar connotations in France and in Britain in the medieval period. It comprised those who exercised some degree of leadership, especially military but also administrative, in medieval society. Anyone who acquired a leading role might be incorporated into this group. Such acquisition might be the result of force, of guile, or of inheritance. General acceptance as a noble by other nobles was sufficient. It is estimated that the nobles formed about the same proportion (between 1 and 2%) of the population in France and in England in the fourteenth or fifteenth century.

As in each country the Crown extended its control over the life of the nation, it came to be more and more accepted that the Crown could approve or determine the criteria for acceptance into the nobility. There was a growing tendancy for such acceptance to be considered legally effective only with the approval (express or tacit) of the Crown or its representatives.

The increasing rigidity of the criteria, which contrasted with the changing nature of society as a whole, and the fact that one of the principal criteria depended on an automatic inheritance of ancestral nobility, meant that eventually the criteria no longer corresponded exclusively to positions of leadership, and it became increasingly the case that the formal criteria of nobility could be satisfied by persons who exercised no particular role in society.

The evolution of the nobility of each country was partly controlled by particular forces derived from the wider history of that country, which tended to graft different characteristics on to the original common basis, and this led to some divergence between the evolutionary paths of the nobilities of the three countries. The divergence between England and France increased in and after the sixteenth century, while that between England and Scotland decreased in and after the seventeenth century.

In England not only has the thing itself evolved, but also its name has undergone a restriction of meaning, at least in general usage, and has come to be applied more particularly, almost exclusively, to the peers who, by the fifteenth century, had come to form a recognisable group within the old nobility, characterised by particular privileges, especially a hereditary personal share in the government of the kingdom. At the same time the term "gentleman", which had once had much the same broad meaning as the term "noble", tended to become more particularly associated with those who were not peers but who belonged to what might previously have been called the nobility.(1)

Accordingly the English group of which we speak is generally referred to, since at least the seventeenth century, as the gentry.(2)

This group has never enjoyed any particular taxation advantages or other substantial privileges. Its members have not been excluded from the practice of any occupation or profession.

While the dignity of gentleman is recognised by English law, the criteria which qualify a person for this dignity have not been the subject of any clear legislative act. However, they have been given some definition by certain judicial acts and certain pronouncements made by or on behalf of the Crown (judgments of the Court of Chivalry, tenor of Visitation Commissions, etc) some of which will be mentioned below. These show that the quality of gentleman can be based on (or proved by) descent or certain posts or dignities, but that this is not essential and that it is possible to base an effective claim to gentility on public repute. This last criterion is reminiscent of the original criterion by which a person who was generally accepted as noble by the other nobles was indeed a noble.

In Scotland there has been an evolution which in some respects has followed what happened in England. With the development of a peerage, the members thereof gradually came to be spoken of as the nobility. In this sense the term did not include Scottish barons. (The lowest rank of the Scottish peerage consisted of "lords" rather than "barons"; the latter term was properly applied to the feudal barons who are mentioned in Chapter 11 and who were liable to be summoned to attend Parliament until relieved of this duty in 1587. The heirs of such barons, or other holders of such baronies, are still entitled to use this title.)

The meaning of the term "gentleman" in Scotland is generally similar to its meaning in England. While the term "noble" is often applied restrictively to peers, it has retained its broader significance in some legal circles. The resistance to the restriction of this term to peers has been evident since the seventeenth century in the writings of Lord Advocate Mackenzie of Rosehaugh, and continues to be found today in the practice of Lyon Court. There has been some use by the latter of the term "noblesse" rather than "nobility" so as to avoid any possibility of misunderstanding.

The criteria of nobility in French law had become fairly clearly defined by the early part of the seventeenth century. They involved long descent within the group, or direct ennoblement by the King, or the tenure of certain posts. The possession of a noble fief, which had for a long time been a principal mode of ennoblement, had lost this power in 1579. Certain taxation and other advantages and privileges were attached to the noble state.

113

These were to some extent counterbalanced by certain disabilities, such as the exclusion of nobles from many lucrative pursuits in commerce and elsewhere on pain of loss of nobility. Within the group there were no legal distinctions of privilege, except in the case of those who were duke-peers. There were certain social and cultural differences which in part were based on differences of wealth, for there were very poor nobles as well as very rich ones. These differences had no legal basis, and do not concern us here.(3)

All French nobles were characterised by the exclusive legal right to the basic noble title of "Ecuyer", which might sometimes be replaced by "Chevalier" (these terms were placed after the surname) or by "Noble" or "Messire" (these terms were placed before the Christian name).(4)

Titles of baron, viscount, count and marquis were occasionally conferred by the King, but these titles, which were normally inherited in accordance with the rule of male primogeniture, were little more than decorations, and were perhaps more nearly equivalent to British baronetcies than to British peerages, whose powers, privileges and status they did not share. More equivalent to British peers were duke-peers ("Ducs et Pairs") who not only had special privileges at Court but could also sit as judges in the Parlement.(5)

For convenience we will continue to use the terms "noble" and "nobility" which are apt to cover the broader groups we have described in all three countries. An important legal and practical difference between the nobilities of France and Britain is to be found in the professions which were open to them. An occupation which was felt to be servile or narrowly commercial might lower the esteem in which a particular British gentleman was held. Such an occupation might extinguish a Frenchman's nobility altogether.

Allegations were made, in some seventeenth century cases in the English Court of Chivalry, that certain persons could not be gentlemen because they had exercised certain occupations. The

Court's reaction to these allegations is not always clear, but there is no evidence that it believed that any honest and lawful occupation was incompatible with gentility. Some cases show that clothiers, soap-boilers and apothecaries were accepted by the court as gentlemen (it was not that these trades actually made their practitioners gentlemen, but if they were gentlemen, they did not cease to be so if they practised these trades).(6)

According to a seventeenth century Scottish institutional writer, nobility may be suspended during the exercise of "mean trades". However, there seems to be no judicial decision on the point. In any event, the disability is said by this writer to cease when the "mean trade" is left off, and then the person concerned returns to his former dignity.(7)

In France there were various occupations which were considered to be incompatible with nobility. The exercise of mechanical arts for commercial purposes fell among them, subject to a number of exceptions one of which was glass making. Servile occupations, such as the tilling of another's land for wages, also fell among them; personally tilling one's own land was permissible and was not unusual among the poorer nobles. The technical term for the loss of nobility as a result of such occupations was "Dérogeance".(8)

"Dérogeance" became effective only when it had been recognised by the authorities, for example when a noble's status was being examined during a nobiliary survey. Many instances were ignored or overlooked by the authorities. Moreover, some of the rules were imprecise or were the subject of regional variations and exceptions. For example, the numerous and often poor nobles of Brittany enjoyed the privilege that the forbidden occupations did not extinguish their nobility but only caused its temporary suspension until they (or their children) gave up such occupations. Until this happened their nobility was said to be "asleep". It has been suggested that in this respect the nobiliary law of Brittany occupied a position midway between that of Britain and that of most of France.(9)

In the case of commerce, there was a substantial difference between the French rules and those of England and Scotland, although the difference was not as great as has sometimes been alleged. It was said in an eighteenth century Scottish birthbrief whose purpose was to attest someone's nobility that he was "pursuing merchandise"; such a statement was hardly likely to be included in a French certificate of nobility. The difference appears to have arisen not only from a feeling that trade was not "noble" but also from the law which, in France but not in England or Scotland, conferred on the nobles both the advantage of certain tax privileges and the disadvantage that they could not enrich themselves by trade. This exclusion was confirmed by a Royal Edict in 1560. However, its effects were moderated, both by local laws and customs and by more general enactments which followed changes in royal policy. In 1629, wishing to encourage the establishment of colonies in the New World, the King declared that nobles could engage in trade by sea. An Edict of 1669, confirmed by another in 1701, and by an Order in Council in 1727, enlarged the permitted area to include wholesale trade within France itself. Later in the eighteenth century the King began to grant Letters Patent of nobility to persons whose merits were actually stated to be the prosperity and other benefits brought by commerce on a large scale.(10)

Notwithstanding the divergences between the evolutionary paths of the nobilities of the three countries, it was recognised in law that there was a basic equivalence between them. This is indicated by the following. A family of English, French or Scottish origin which was transplanted into one of the other two countries, and which thus acquired a new nationality, was admitted into the nobility of its new country if it could prove that it had been noble in its country of origin. Such admittance was in several instances the subject of a formal decision by the competent authorities.(11)

It was in France (where the enjoyment of certain privileges and posts depended on the possession of nobility) that the likelihood was greatest of a noble family finding itself in circumstances which made it desirable or necessary for it to make formal proof of its nobility before one of the competent authorities, such as the Juge d'Armes, the Royal Genealogist, the commissioners carrying out nobiliary surveys, and so forth. There were many families of English or Scottish origin who settled in France in the seventeenth and eighteenth centuries, and who were accepted by these authorities as forming part of the French nobility by reason of their previous noble status in England or Scotland. It was considered that those who were in this position were entitled as of right to Royal Letters Patent recognising them as French nobles.(12)

That long descent in the English or Scottish nobility or gentry was equivalent to long descent in the French nobility is emphasised by the cases of persons who were admitted to posts or privileges which required ancient nobility. In 1775 the son of one Scottish emigrant was admitted among the Pages of the Royal Stables, for which the minimum qualification, as re-defined earlier in the eighteenth century, was uninterrupted noble status since before 1550. In 1787 a descendant of another Scottish family, which had settled in France at about the beginning of the seventeenth century, was admitted to Court Honours, for which the minimum qualification was uninterrupted noble status since before 1400.(13)

A French family of foreign origin did not lose its nobility by reason of any breach of the French rules which it might have committed before it became French, provided that such "breach" was not contrary to the nobiliary laws of its country of origin. At one time this was not clear, and some of the earlier Royal Letters Patent confirming the nobility of Frenchmen of English or Scottish origin contained a clause explicitly absolving them of any "Dérogeance" which they might have incurred, while others recited that the beneficiary's nobility had been preserved in spite of the trade in which he had engaged, because such trade was not incompatible with nobility in his ancestral country. Then in 1668 an Order in Council made it clear that French nobles of foreign origin were not to be deprived of their nobility by reason of any trade carried out by their ancestors who had settled in France, provided that such trade was permitted to nobles in their country of origin.(14)

In England where, since the Visitations ended in the seventeenth century, there has been no obligation to prove one's nobility, there seem to be few published records of persons being officially confirmed as members of the English gentry because they possessed French or Scottish nobility. The clearest instances are perhaps to be found in the Visitation records, where a number of families which had arrived more or less recently from France or Scotland appear to have been accepted as gentle, and to have had their arms entered, because of their previous status and possession of arms. One family appears to have had its arms entered at the Visitation of London in 1633-1635 on the basis of a certificate of Pierre d'Hozier, who was then a French herald and who later became Juge d'Armes, to the effect that the family was noble and bore the arms. The arms of another family were entered on the basis of a certificate from the Lord Lyon to the effect that the person concerned was descended from a second son of a family which bore certain ancient arms (duly differenced by a second son's crescent). Another person had his French ancestry entered with the note: "The Armes respited until he can send into France where his ancestors remained".(15)

There are a number of more recent confirmations by the English Kings of Arms of arms borne by families in France or Scotland before they became English. The recognition of the right of these families to bear arms amounts to a recognition of their gentility (since, according to the Court of Chivalry, arms are lawfully borne only by gentlemen). Moreover, the recognition that they are entitled to bear, as English arms, the arms they bore when they were French or Scottish families appears to be a recognition that their English gentility is derived from their former French or Scottish gentility or nobility.(16)

The position in Scotland appears to be somewhat analogous to that in England. The arms of English persons who settle in Scotland are accepted and matriculated in Lyon Register, and this amounts to a reception of such persons into the Scottish gentry or noblesse (since, according to the Lord Lyon, arms are lawfully borne in Scotland only by nobles). Those who could establish that they are in lawful possession of French nobility and arms would presumably be treated in the same way.(17)

The use of arms originated among the nobles of Western Europe and between the eleventh and thirteenth centuries such use became increasingly wide-spread for the purpose of identifying the nobles in war and other military exploits such as tournaments (on shields and banners) and in peace (on seals and garments).

The ways in which arms are mentioned in "official" documents of the fifteenth and sixteenth centuries (especially in certain royal grants in which they are associated with nobility or in which they are said to be signs of nobility; in the oaths and ordinances governing the activities of medieval heralds and in Visitation commissions and the resulting orders and disclaimers; all of which have been alluded to in Chapters 5 and 9) suggest that the royal authority assumed that there was a necessary connection between arms and nobility, to the extent that those who were noble and those who bore arms formed a single category.

Yet it is known that, at least in some parts of France, there were many non-nobles who identified themselves by means of armorial seals in deeds executed in that period. There seem to be no records of legal action against non-nobles who used arms on seals or otherwise. It has been argued that this state of affairs shows that it was lawful for non-nobles to use arms. Opponents of this view have argued that if the non-nobles who used arms were not penalised this was not because their acts were lawful but because the authorities (in the areas where such use took place) were too weak to enforce the law, or felt it unnecessary to do so.

We will now look a little more closely at the legal situation in each country, in so far as it may be deduced from any relevant statutes, orders or commissions from the Crown or its authorised officers, and from any relevant judicial decisions. It will be seen that, however vague the legal situation may have been in earlier times, it later became much clearer and firmer.

The nobiliary aspect of the English Visitations in the sixteenth and seventeenth centuries has been briefly discussed in Chapter 9, where the inter-relationship of arms and gentility in the Sovereign's Commissions and in the operation of the surveys has been pointed out. That the usurping of the title of gentleman was contrary to the English laws of arms was confirmed by the Court of Chivalry in 1635 in a case involving a man who had been proclaimed no gentleman during a Visitation.(18)

One could be a gentleman without possessing arms. This is suggested by some Visitation records, where it seems that some families were entered without any arms. It is confirmed by the records of the Court of Chivalry, which show that the court was prepared to accept that certain posts or offices, or merely the possession of a general reputation that one is a gentleman, are sufficient to establish gentility in law.(19)

It was necessary to be a gentleman in order to be qualified to bear arms. The Court of Chivalry, which has an exclusive jurisdiction in matters relating both to gentility and to arms, has accepted that arms are "ensigns of gentry" and that arms can be lawfully borne only if the bearer is a gentleman.(20)

Examination of the acts of the English Kings of Arms seems to show that from early times they have in general behaved in conformity with the law as it later came to be applied by the Court of Chivalry. The English Kings of Arms have been certifying arms to individuals since the fifteenth century (at least). It is possible to take the view that even in the earliest times their Letters Patent did not so much ennoble their recipients as recognise that the latter had already achieved nobility and provide them with a grant or a confirmation of the appropriate "ensigns" of nobility, that is, arms. This is consistent with the view expressed in the fifteenth century by Upton, whose statement that arms could be either assumed or granted by a herald is clearly predicated on the person concerned having previously become noble, apparently by reason of his conduct or style of life. And whereas royal grants often contained explicit clauses granting nobility as well as arms (see Chapter 5), grants from the Kings of

Arms were worded differently, and often seem to imply only that the Kings of Arms were empowered to recognise both old and new nobility and to mark it with its appropriate sign, which is arms.(21)

One of the more explicit of the earlier grants was made in 1450 by Garter. It states that the grantee is worthy of being admitted among the other ancient gentle and noble men ("anciens gentils et nobles hommes") and, for remembrance of his gentility ("gentillesse"), Garter has devised and assigned to him certain arms. Some late fifteenth and early sixteenth century grants from the English Kings of Arms contain similar passages, or state that virtuous men should be known by tokens of honour and nobility (that is, a shield of arms, helm and crest), that the grantee, who is a "gentilhomme", has merited that "in all places of honour" he and his posterity should be admitted among "the other ancient gentle and noble men", and that, for remembrance of his good repute, they have devised and assigned to him certain arms. Analogous forms of words appear in other grants of this period.(22)

As will be mentioned below, such passages also appear in many grants made after the events of 1530, which we are about to consider.

Reference has been made in Chapter 5 to a dispute which arose in the early part of the sixteenth century between two of the English Kings of Arms and which caused Henry VIII to threaten that he would no longer allow them to meddle in the granting of arms. In the course of this dispute, which came to a head in 1530, one King of Arms (Clarenceux) alleged that another (Garter) had acted against "the honour of noble men and of all gentlemen of name and of arms" by giving arms "to bound men to vile persons not able to uphold the honour of noblesse". Garter denied this allegation, stating that he had complied with the customs and usages according to which "every person being of good name and fame and good renown and not vile born or rebels might be admitted to be ennobled to have arms, having lands and possessions of free tenure to the yearly value of ten pounds sterling or in movable goods three hundred pounds sterling". Clarenceux said that Garter had no authority to "give any arms or grant of noblesse" but he believed that he himself and Norroy did have such authority. Clarenceux claimed that the King was so displeased with Garter's behaviour that he discharged all the Kings of Arms of their authority "of giving of arms or cognizances of arms to ennoble any person". However, the King relented.(23)

It was in 1530 that Henry VIII issued the Letters Patent constituting a Commission of Visitation in favour of Clarenceux which are mentioned in Chapters 5 and 9. In this document the King refers to arms as "tokens of nobleness" and orders that all who shall be "ennobled" by a grant of arms are "to have their arms registered in the Earl Marshal's book".(24)

Royal Letters Patent appointing a new Norroy in 1536 gave him authority "tam aptandi dandi et concedendi insignia arma et cristas caeteraque nobilitatis monumenta quam visitandi et corrigendi insignia vitiosa et alia delicta arma vel nobilitatem concernentia".(25)

Some of the grants made by the English Kings of Arms in the sixteenth century (after 1530) continued to refer more or less explicitly to the connection between arms and nobility (or gentility). Of these grants, many employed terms similar to those mentioned above in connection with some grants made before 1530, referring for example to the grantee having deserved to be admitted among other noble or gentle men, or to his nobility being commemorated by the grant of arms.(26)

In the seventeenth century there were some grants which mentioned that arms were tokens of gentility or honour, or that the grantee was enrolled among the nobles or the gentry. By then the term "gentry", already widely used in the sixteenth century, had almost completely replaced "nobility" in relation to those who were not peers, although a reference to arms being "ensigns of nobility" is found in a grant made as late as 1726.(27)

Some eighteenth century grants of arms begin with a passage on the following lines: "Whereas those ancient badges and ensigns of gentility, ... known by the name of arms ... are ... conferred upon deserving persons to distinguish them from the common sort of people, who neither can, nor may pretend to use them without lawful authority ...". The latest such grant which we have noticed was made in 1768.(28)

The English Kings of Arms are, as we have seen in Chapter 4, officers of the Earl Marshal, and they act under his authority, which was confirmed by Charles II in 1673, as being that of the officer immediately under the Sovereign for determining and ordering all matters touching arms, ensigns of nobility, honour and chivalry. In addition to approving all grants made by the Kings of Arms in the last three centuries, the Earl Marshal has himself referred, in the course of his ministerial duties, to a connection existing between arms and nobility or gentility. An early instance is found in certain rules as to fees which were to be charged in the first half of the sixteenth century by the Kings of Arms "when they shall ennoble any person with arms". A later instance occurred in an Earl Marshal's warrant of 1687 authorising the Kings of Arms to grant arms to a particular person; in this document arms are described as "so signal a badge of gentility".(29)

It seems that since the latter part of the eighteenth century no English grant of arms has contained any explicit reference to nobility or gentility.

What is required of someone before he can qualify for a grant of arms in England has been defined at various times. Garter's view of 1530 has already been mentioned. It agreed fairly well with the "Ordinances of the Duke of Clarence", dating from some time in the fifteenth century, which said that arms were not to be given to any vile or dishonest person, but only to those who were virtuous, honest and of good substance. The royal Letters Patent of 1530 in favour of Clarenceux authorised him to grant arms to persons "by the service done to us or to other that be increased or augmented to possessions and riches able to maintain the

123

same, so that they be not issued of vile blood, rebels to our person nor heretics contrary to the faith, but men of good honest reputation". Royal Letters Patent of 1618 appointing commissioners to carry out the office of Earl Marshal stated that arms were not to be granted to "persons of base birth or of mean vocation and quality of living". Enquiries have sometimes been made, or evidence called for, to establish that petitioners for arms could indeed live as gentlemen; there are explicit references to this in some grants made in the latter part of the seventeenth century and in the early part of the eighteenth century.(30)

The qualification of a grantee of arms is epitomised in the royal Letters Patent appointing each new King of Arms, which empowers him to grant arms to "eminent men". (This term ("claris viri") first appeared in Letters Patent of 1536.) This places on the Kings of Arms a duty, which was acknowledged by them in a Return made to the House of Commons in 1863, to ensure that no applicant for arms is to be entertained unless he occupies "a fit station in life for such distinction". The reponsibility of the Kings of Arms to see that grantees of arms are of sufficient excellence and merit has been re-stated by a contemporary English herald.(31)

Whether, as has been suggested, the English Kings of Arms do not in strict law make non-noble persons into noble or gentle persons but only "recognise" existing nobility or gentility, or whether (as some of the cited passages might indicate) they can of their own power effect this "transformation", the practical effect is the same.

If a King of Arms makes a grant to someone who is no gentleman, he may perhaps himself be guilty of a breach of duty, which might be justiciable in the Court of Chivalry (as was attempted in a case in 1638). However, if the grant is made with the approval of the Earl Marshal, as has been the invariable rule for the last three centuries, it is difficult to see how it could be challenged in the Court of Chivalry. Accordingly it may be said that someone who has received a grant of arms is undoubtedly a gentleman in law.(32)

It has been recognised in modern times, by Judges of the courts both in England and in Scotland, that the bearing of arms is a dignity.(33)

In Scotland, the legal significance of the bearing of arms is the subject of statutory authority. The significance of earlier statutes may be somewhat vague, as with an Act of Parliament of 1430 from which it appears that every freeholder was expected to possess a seal of his arms, while it appears that every freeholder was considered to be the peer of a knight.(34)

The import of later statutes is clearer. In the Act of 1592 there is mention of "gentlemen of blood" and those descended of "noble stock and lineage", who are clearly understood to be qualified to bear arms. On the other hand there are the "common sort of people" who are "not worthy by the law of arms to bear any ensigns armorial", and the Act affirms the Lord Lyon's power to forbid them to presume to use arms.(35)

According to Mackenzie of Rosehaugh, the institutional author and Lord Advocate, who wrote after the 1592 Act but before the 1672 Act, Lyon could give arms only to such as were noble by descent, because this followed from the 1592 Act. Lyon could not "nobilitate" someone who was not noble, and therefore could not bestow on such a person "the marks of nobility". Mackenzie contrasted this with the powers of the King, who could bestow arms on anyone he chose.(36)

The Act of 1672 defines three categories of armorial offender. Two come within the group of "noblemen, barons and gentlemen"; they are qualified to bear arms, and their offence is, in one category, that they bear the undifferenced arms of their chief, or, in the second category, that they bear arms which are not derived from their predecessors. The third category does not come within the group of "noblemen, barons and gentlemen" and its members are therefore not qualified to bear arms at all, they evidently are what the Act of 1592 called "people not worthy by the law of arms to bear any ensigns armorial".(37)

Since 1663 the Letters Patent creating each Lord Lyon have empowered him to grant arms to "virtuous and well-deserving persons", and this power was confirmed by the Act of 1672.(38)

According to Mackenzie, the "virtue" which qualifies a person for a grant of arms is not a moral quality but a public or "civil" quality. Those who have it include barons, persons who hold land directly of the crown, soldiers having "considerable command", clergymen, doctors of universities, advocates, physicians, orators and "laureate poets". They have the quality of "gentlemen". Mere possession of wealth is not in itself a qualification. Nor is poverty a disqualification, even when long continued. The calling of merchant does not of itself ennoble, but it is not said to be incompatible with nobility. On the other hand the exercise of mean trades ("viles et mechanicas artes") suspends the right to arms.(39)

Scottish patents of arms do not seem to have contained explicit references to nobility or gentility until relatively recently. However, Lyon has been issuing certificates of nobility or "birthbriefs" for some centuries and in some seventeenth and eighteenth as well as twentieth century examples the nobiliary status of the person concerned has been explicitly described. Such nobiliary status appears to have depended primarily on armorial status. In some certificates Lyon referred to his sphere of duty as including the control of the arms of "peers, prelates, barons and other nobles" of Scotland, from which it is seen that nobles included not only peers, bishops and feudal barons but also "other nobles", that is gentlemen.(40)

A modern Lord Lyon has stated "with full official weight" that a patent of arms is "a Diploma of Nobility" and that a coat of arms is "the outward indication of nobility". Modern Scottish grants of arms state in relation to the recipient that "by demonstration of which Ensigns Armorial he and his successors in the same are, amongst all Nobles and in all Places of Honour, to be taken, numbered, accounted and received as Nobles in the Noblesse of Scotland". While the granted arms can be borne undifferenced only by the grantee and each successive heir, all others within the destination are considered to be noble and to be entitled as of right to matriculate a differenced version of the arms.(41)

The English and Scottish laws are similar in that in both the lawful possession of arms is proof of possession of nobility or gentility; moreover this proof is normally made by putting forward either a grant of arms or an official recording of arms (for example in English Visitations or in Scottish matriculations) or evidence of immemorial possession of arms. French law was different in that, in the post-medieval period, non-nobles could lawfully possess arms (although not timbred arms), and in that proof of nobility was not normally made by means of grants of arms or official recordings of arms or long possession of arms.

Whether it was lawful for non-nobles to bear arms in France in medieval times is difficult to say. The evidence is perhaps inconclusive. However that may be, there is no doubt that in later times the bearing of arms by non-nobles was lawful. Reference has been made in Chapter 11 to various legal enactments and judicial decisions in the sixteenth century and later, which imposed penalties on non-nobles who used timbred arms. Accordingly, while some French writers on heraldry in the seventeenth century continued to claim that non-nobles were not entitled to bear arms, it was only the bearing of timbred arms which was illegal.

Any remaining doubts could not survive the Armorial Général of 1696-1709, which has been considered in Chapter 9. The Edict which created the Armorial Général allowed the registration of a shield of arms by anyone who fell within a definition which was so wide that it covered large numbers of non-nobles. For the avoidance of any possible doubt, it was stated in the Edict that the certificates which were to be given to those whose arms were to be registered would not be evidence of nobility. In fact, the majority of the persons in whose names arms were registered were not noble.

It is little wonder that in 1760, when the King attempted to restrict the lawful bearing of arms to certain categories of persons (who even then would have included many non-nobles) the Parlement condemned this as being contrary to the custom of the Kingdom, and the King abandoned his attempt.

All this was without prejudice to the rule, which remained law although it was increasingly broken by many bourgeois wishing to give themselves an air, that only nobles were entitled to bear timbred arms.

It has been indicated in Chapter 5 that every French royal grant of arms seems to have been made with or following a royal grant of nobility, or to someone who was (or was believed by the King to be) already noble. Accordingly, a royal grant of arms might be adequate proof of nobility.(42)

However, the number of such grants was so small that only a tiny proportion of the nobles could have proved their nobility in this way. In post-medieval France there was no one apart from the King himself who could make grants of arms. In particular, it will be recalled that the settlements of the Juge d'Armes were not the same as grants. Moreover, while such settlements included (or at least were supposed to include) a timbre only if the beneficiary was noble, there seems to be no sign that the courts or any other authority treated them as evidence of nobility.

When a French noble wished or was required to prove his nobility, for example in the nobiliary surveys of the seventeenth century or in the other circumstances described in Chapter 9, he usually did so, not by showing that he possessed arms (whether timbred or not), but by proving either that he had been ennobled by Royal Letters Patent or by the tenure of an ennobling post, or that he was descended from someone who had been ennobled in this way, or that his ancestors had for several generations enjoyed the titles and privileges of nobility.

This does not mean that arms were of little importance to French nobles. The earlier chapters have shown how often arms and nobility were juxtaposed. The nobles continued to regard the use of arms by non-nobles as an abuse, long after it had clearly become lawful. Nearly all French litigation over arms seems to have involved nobility in some way. Most cases related to the bearing of arms by members of noble families, or to the usurping of "noble" arms by non-nobles (either by taking the arms of a noble family, or by giving their own arms a spurious noble appearance by means of a timbre).

Although not confined to the nobility, the bearing of arms remained in some ways an honourable distinction, which could be lost. It was not only that loss of nobility could lead to the loss of the right to use timbred arms; even the non-noble's right to untimbred arms could be lost. A conviction for a crime judged to be infamous might be followed by a sentence of deprivation of arms (if the culprit was noble, he might be deprived of his nobility as well). A Royal Declaration of 1635 provided that those who left the army without permission might be deprived of the right to bear any arms. A Royal Edict of 1679 provided that persons guilty of duelling might be deprived of their arms. It appears that the resulting inability to bear arms might be transmitted to the children of a person punished in this way, or at least that the children might have to replace the arms of their ancestors by new ones.(43)

It is possible to regard this as a continuing reflection of an association between arms and "noble behaviour", if not legal nobility. It is reminiscent of certain practices in Britain. For example, it has been said that in Scotland a conviction for treason abolishes the right to bear arms. When a person was forfeited in the Scottish parliament, the Lord Lyon defaced his arms as a sign that he was ignoble and had lost the ability to bear arms. In England, the requirement that one must be a gentleman in order to be qualified to bear arms seems to imply that if someone ceased to be a gentleman (which presumably is a matter on which the Court of Chivalry could pronounce), he would lose his right to bear arms.(44)

That the French revolutionaries believed that there was a connection between nobility and arms is indicated by the fact that they abolished them together. On 19 June 1790 the Assembly issued a decree which abolished hereditary nobility and forbade the use of arms by anyone. Four days later the King issued Letters Patent approving the decree. In 1791 a law was passed prescribing that those who used arms were to be fined and would lose their civic rights. Other laws followed which were intended to obliterate all traces of the feudal past, especially after the "abolition" of the monarchy in 1792. In particular, a decree of August 1793 ordered the confiscation of all buildings and enclosures decorated with arms.(45)

In the nineteenth century, the use of arms ceased to be illegal in France. After some zigzags under the empires and monarchies which succeeded each other, French law came eventually to regard arms merely as symbols of the person or family who used them. Their use was quite unregulated except that if the arms associated with a family were "stolen" by a third party, the members of the family could bring an action in the courts to restrain the third party from continuing to use the arms.(46)

This is still the legal position in France.

Accordingly, modern France has no law of arms, and differs in this respect from modern Britain, where the laws of arms of England and Scotland continue to be part of the laws of each of these countries.(47)

NOTES TO CHAPTERS

Chapter 1 - Introduction

(1)   Cherin (1788), 33; X (1900), 44-45; Heraldica (1940), 132; Innes (1941A), 129; Wagner (1956), 63-64.

Chapter 2 - Legislation

(1)   The relevant portion of the Declaration of 1673 / Order in Council of 1674 has been printed in, for example, Squibb (1959), 79-80. For examples of Visitation Commissions, see Observations (1724), 50-51; Dallaway (1793), 309-315; X (1900), 120-125; Armytage (1910), vii-x; Wagner (1956), 9-10. The Letters Patent of James I, Charles II and James II in favour of the Earl Marshal are available in X (1900), 68-86; Full Report (1955), 63-64; Squibb (1959), 239-240. With regard to Letters Patent creating new Kings of Arms, see X (1900), 100-108; Wagner (1956), 98-99.

        Several relevant documents are printed in Squibb (1985).

(2)   Extracts or summaries of most of these particular laws are to be found, arranged chronologically, in Cherin (1788) and its reprinted versions. Much of this material was already available in D'Hozier (1738-1768) I, Second Part. With regard to the Ordinance of 1556, see Prinet (1917). The full text of the Edict of 1696 appears, for example, in Cadot (1697), 41-145; Meurgey de Tupigny (1965-1967) I, viii-xii; some of the subsequent legislation is in the following pages of Meurgey de Tupigny (who also gives the text of the abortive law of 1760 which is discussed in Chapter 9).

(3)   The texts of the Acts of Parliament of 1592, 1672 and 1867 are readily available; see Act (1592); Act (1672); Act (1867). For some of the other Acts see Act (1669); Seton (1863), 495-498; Stevenson (1914), 437-439; Bruce (1980), 16. For some Letters Patent creating new Lords Lyon, see Mackenzie (1680), 8; Seton (1863), 490-493; Stevenson (1914), 451-455.

Chapter 3 - The Judiciary

(1)   Our account of the Court of Chivalry is based mainly on Squibb (1959), passim; also X (1900), 61, 68-87; P (1955), 133-153; Full Report (1955), passim; Wagner (1956), 21, 24, 122; Squibb (1981), 448, 477, 478.

(2)   Squibb (1981), 477 (superseding Squibb (1959), 221-224; Full Report (1955) 36, 52).

131

(3)   P (1955), 141; Full Report (1955), 11, 12, 15, 24-27; Squibb (1959), 96-102, 153.

(4)   Full Report (1955), 16-17.

(5)   Nisbet (1722-1742) II, Part IV, 69-70, 74-75.

(6)   Act (1592); Act (1669); Act (1672); Seton (1863), 45-50; Nichols (1865), 393-406; Act (1867); Nichols (1867), 80-86 (where Lyon Clerk is said to be appointed by Lyon; this was the older practice ended by the 1867 Act); Stevenson (1914), 89-98, 445-446; (1926), 2-7; Innes (1930), 332, 333, 336-341; Heraldica (1942), 95; Grant (1945), Introduction; Walker (1963) 487; Innes and Innes (1978), 7-11, 43-44, 106, 116; Brooke-Little (1978), 261.

(7)   Act (1672); Clarke (1916-1917), 255-256; Innes (1930), 339-341; (1941A), 131-132; Heraldica (1940), 131; Innes and Innes (1978), 49, 51, 60-62, 64-67, 75-76. In so far as they are merely temporary privileges without transmissible rights, the bearing of the arms by a spouse or by a daughter, and the bearing thereof with a label by the heir or with other minor cadency marks by unmarried sons, do not require the intervention of the Lord Lyon. Nor is such intervention required to enable two spouses to bear impaled or accollee arms, as this too is a temporary privilege.

(8)   Seton (1863), 21; Nichols (1865), 400; (1867), 82; Stevenson (1914), 69-76; (1926), 3; Innes (1929), 560; (1930), 341-343; (1940A), 255, 257; (1940E), 182-183, 186, 188; Heraldica (1942), 92, 94; Walker (1963), 187; Innes and Innes (1978), 8, 10, 117.

(9)   Innes (1930), 342-343; (1940A), 293; (1940E), 182, 186, 188; P (1955), 147-149; Full Report (1955), 17-18, 41-42, 54, 56-57; Walker (1963), 187; Innes and Innes (1978), 52, 63-65; Brooke-Little (1978), 124; Squibb (1981), 442, 448, 463, 477, 478; Dennys (1982), 19.

(10)   Mathieu (1946), 56, 106, 123, 143, 144. Brief notes on these courts are in Marion (1923), 32-33.

(11)   Brief notes on the various sovereign courts are in Marion (1923), 137-138, 422-433.

(12)   Bouvot (1628) II, 46-47, 718-720; Geliot and Palliot (1661), 371; Brillon (1711) I, 155-156; II, 786-792; La Roche Flavin and Graverol (1745), 613-615; Cherin (1788), 357-359; Maugard (1788), 291-292; Mathieu (1946), 57-58, 70, 104, 123, 144-145, 150.

(13)   Cherin (1788), 358-359; Maugard (1788), 109-110, 291-292; Mathieu (1946), 60. Brief notes on the Cour des Aides are in Marion (1923), 156-157.

(14)   Cherin (1788), 220-223, 227-228; Mathieu (1946), 59, 84-85.

(15)   Cherin (1788), 91-93; Maugard (1788), 89, 194-196; Mathieu (1946), 57, 70-73, 76, 123, 139; Sereville and Saint Simon (1975), 54; Grolée-Virville (1978), 17-19.

(16)   Cherin (1788), 93; Marion (1923), 129-130, 336, 543; Mathieu (1946), 59-60, 70; Meyer (1972), 302-305; Grolée-Virville (1978), 19. In the sixteenth century the Court of the Constable and Marshals of France had jurisdiction over lawsuits involving the heralds in their personal capacity (Figon (1580), 31 vo.).

(17)   Innes (1940E), 185, 194, 210-213; (1946), 127; Full Report (1955), 57; Squibb (1956), 6, 12; Innes and Innes (1978), 96-100.

(18)   Scohier (1597), 36-37; Vulson de La Colombière (1838), 424-425; Du Roure de Paulin (1906), 11-12; Mathieu (1946), 67-68, 259-260.

Chapter 4 – The Officers of Arms

(1)   Belleval (1867), 529-540; Grant (1945), Introduction; Mathieu (1946), 61-66; Wagner (1967), 1-122; Galbreath and Jéquier (1977), 57-62.

(2)   Le Feron (1555), 27-28vo., 39vo.-40vo.; Fauchet (1606), 25vo.; Maugard (1788), 198; Leber (1838), 116, 118; Vulson de La Colombière (1838), 396-397, 403, 407, 432; Vallet de Viriville (1866), 5, 14; Du Roure de Paulin (1906), 18-19, 34-35; Wagner (1956), 36-37, 63; London (1970), 90, 94.

(3)   Le Feron (1555), 28; Signac (1559), e.i.-g.i.; Fauchet (1606), 25-28; Favyn (1620) I, 53-54, 64; II, 1845-1865; Leber (1838), 116-118; Vulson de La Colombière (1838), 396-398, 409-410; Martres (1847), 365-366; Vallet de Viriville (1866), 5-6; Du Roure de Paulin (1906), 7, 15, 19-20, 55-57; Wagner (1956), 41, 54; (1967), 46-48.

(4)   Vulson de La Colombière (1838), 409-410, 418; Howard and Chester (1883), 400; Du Roure de Paulin (1906), 17; Meurgey de Tupigny (1965-1967) I, 37; II, 271; III, 403; IV, 89.

(5)   Fox-Davies (1949), 29-38; London (1952); Wagner and London (1963), passim; Wagner (1967), passim; Brooke-Little (1969), Note 6; Squibb (1981), 446-447; (1985), 68-127; Dennys (1982), 144-150.

(6)   Dickson (1877), cxci-cxcvii, ccxcii-ccxcvi; Stevenson (1914), 39-40, 445-455; Innes (1930), 329, 338; Grant (1945); London and Wagner (1949), 92-104; Wagner (1967), 20, 23; Innes and Innes (1978), 4-7, 9.

(7)   Le Feron (1555), 31 vo.-32; Fauchet (1606), 26 vo.; Favyn (1620) I, 59; Edmondson (1780) I, 125-130, 136, 140-141; Dallaway (1793), 84-85; Vulson de La Colombière (1838), 400; Seton (1863), 25-30; Dickson (1877), cxcv-cxcvii; Du Roure de Paulin (1906), 7; Grant (1945); London and Wagner (1949), 43, 47-49; Squibb (1967H); (1981), 447; Innes and Innes (1978), 10.

(8)   Le Peron (1555), 1-1 vo.; Moreau (1630), 13; Maugard (1788), 203; Vulson de La Colombière (1838), 432-435; Wagner (1956), 42, 57, 61; (1967), 39, 47.

(9)   Seton (1863), 29; Stevenson (1914), 41, 86-87; Innes (1930), 350; Brooke-Little (1978), 261. Lyon's immediate relationship to the Sovereign and his functions as an Officer of State in marshalling Scottish coronations and other ceremonies, are no doubt among the reasons why he has for centuries enjoyed the style of "Lord Lyon" (Innes (1930), 330-331; Grant (1945), Introduction; Innes and Innes (1978), 4-5).

(10)   Observations (1724), 47-49; Edmondson (1780) I, 143-146, 151-153; Squibb (1959), 79-80; (1981), 448; (1985), 60-63, 97-105, 123-126; Wagner (1967), 120, 188-198, 275-280, 334; Brooke-Little (1969), Notes 5, 12, 215; Dennys (1982), 137-139.

(11)   See Note 10, and Baildon (1904) (July), 53-56; Squibb (1959), 107; (1981), 442, 446; Dennys (1982), 149. The quoted passage in the last sentence of this paragraph is taken from Halsbury's Laws of England (Squibb (1981), 448).

(12)   Wagner (1967), 209, 266. More recently, there was an equally unsuccessful attempt to regulate some incidental aspects of the activities of the College of Arms (College of Arms Bill (1973)).

(13)   Nisbet (1722-1742) II, Part IV, 171-172; Nichols (1867), 80-86 (where the Lyon Clerk is said to be appointed by Lyon; this was the older procedure); Stevenson (1914), 39-41, 46, 441-442; (1926), 1; Innes (1930), 329-338; Fox-Davies (1949), 39-46; Walker (1963), 187; Brooke-Little (1969), Note 10; Innes and Innes (1978), 4-7, 9, 45.

(14)   Act (1592); Act (1672); Mackenzie (1680), 7-8, 11; Seton (1863), 43-45, 51-52; Paul (1903), xi-xiv; Stevenson (1914), 63-64, 77-78; 81, 436-443, 451-455; Innes (1930), 335-336; Walker (1963), 187; Innes and Innes (1978), 122-124.

(15)   Act (1867).

(16)   Heraldica (1942), 100; Innes and Innes (1978), 6. The quoted passage is from Green's Encyclopaedia of the Laws of Scotland (Innes (1930), 337).

(17)   Cadot (1697), 48-49; Edmondson (1780) I, 134; Maugard (1788), 88-89; Vallet de Viriville (1866), 6; Du Roure de Paulin (1906), 11; Mathieu (1947), 66-68; Adam-Even (1957), 31 Contamine (1976), 31; Grolée-Virville (1978), 2.

(18)   Le Feron (1555), 1vo., 4vo., 45; Fauchet (1606), 26; Favyn (1620) I, 56-61; Moreau (1630), 16; Geliot (1635), 220; Maugard (1788), 80; Vulson de La Colombière (1838), 404-406, 418; Du Roure de Paulin (1906), 8-9, 12, 15-20; Mathieu (1946), 68-70; Bluche and Durye (1962) I, 44; Meurgey de Tupigny (1965-1967) I, 37; II, 271; III, 403; IV, 89; Durye (1974), 12-13.

(19)   Vulson de La Colombière (1838),4 04-405; Du Roure de Paulin (1906), 8-9, 18.

(20)   Cherin (1788), 78, 193, 242-243, 354-355; Durye (1974), 3, 6, 14; Sereville and Saint Simon (1975), 53.

(21)   Magneney (1633), 143; Cadot (1697), 54, 57; Cherin (1788), 91-93, 221; Howard and Chester (1883), 100; Du Boscq de Beaumont (1906), 165-166; Mathieu (1946), 70-73, 138-139; Sereville and Saint Simon (1975), 54; Grolée-Virville (1978), 18-19, 89-90, 93, Plate VIII.

(22)   Cherin (1788), 91-93.

(23)   Cherin (1788), 253, 288-289; Mathieu (1946), 72, 87; Meurgey de Tupigny (1965-1967) I, xix-xx; Grolée-Virville (1978), 39-40, 126.

(24)   Cherin (1788), 289; Du Boscq de Beaumont (1906), 174-175; Mathieu (1946), 72; Meurgey de Tupigny (1965-1967) I, xix-xx.

(25)   Cherin (1788), 289; Du Boscq de Beaumont (1906), 174; Mathieu (1946), 72, 87; Meurgey de Tupigny (1965-1967) I, xix-xx.

Chapter 5 – Grants of Arms

(1)   Nichols (1863), 135-137; Watson (1898), 79; X (1900), 50-52; Rylands (1902), 35; Mathieu (1946), 171; Hope and Wagner (1953), 67-68; Wagner (1956), 65-67, 123; Galbreath and Jéquier (1977), 54, 76.

(2)   Littledale (1926), 217-219; Hope and Wagner (1953), 67-68; Wagner (1956), 67.

(3)   Howard (1876), 121-122; (1877), 475-476; Woodward and Burnett (1892), 750-751; X (1900), 56-57, 86-87; Stevenson (1914), 130; Clarke (1920-1922), 235-236; Littledale (1925), 10-11, 48, 89-90, 101-103, 109-111; (1926), 150-151, 163-164, 189-190, 202-203; Fox-Davies (1949), 589; Wagner (1956), 67; (1967), 30; Scott-Giles (1960), 51, 55-56.

(4)   Quicherat (1841-1845) V, 342-346; Rivoire de La Batie (1867), 97, 608; Mathieu (1946), 171-172, 183. The story of the grant of arms to the two woodmen seems to rest on "tradition" only.

(5)   Pastoret (1811-1840) XVII, 98-99; XVIII, 58-59, 192-193; XIX, 556-558. At about the time he granted nobility and arms to Joan of Arc's companion, Charles VII made a grant of nobility to Joan herself and her brothers; no arms are mentioned in the Letters Patent (a copy of which in Du Lis (1856), 94-98, is believed to be genuine, according to H.Morel, La Noblesse de la Famille de Jeanne d'Arc (1972), 9-10 (Société d'Histoire du Droit, Collection d'Histoire Institutionnelle et Sociale 4)). Joan herself stated at her trial that her brothers had been given arms by the King (Quicherat (1841-1845) I, 117-118), and in certain Letters Patent of Louis XIII in 1612 it was acknowledged that she had received the special privilege of bearing the fleur-de-lys, and that her arms had been "granted and depicted" (Du Lis (1856), 100). However, there seems to be no trace of any formal grant of arms to Joan or to her brothers.

(6)   Pastoret (1811-1840) XVIII, 59; Quicherat (1841-1845) V, 345-346; Mathieu (1946), 184-185; Blanc (1975), 542, 547-548.

(7)   Bacquet (1744), 345-346.

(8)   Favyn (1620) I, 27-28; La Roque (1734). Noblesse, 91 (seventeenth century); Nichols (1863), 133; Sauvage (1925), 320; Mathieu (1946), 183-184; Blanc (1975), 546; Arundel de Condé (1981), 40, 43-44. An example of Letters Patent granting an "augmentation of honour" is in Du Lis (1856), 99-106; this grant was made by Louis XIII in 1612.

(9)   Cherin (1788), 288-289; Nichols (1863), 133; Mathieu (1946), 172, 182, 186; Harmon (1977), 118-119. An Example of a royal grant of nobility of 1726 permitting the bearing of the ancient arms of the family as approved by the Juge d'Armes is printed in Daigre, Armorial Général et Universal (1907-1909) II, sub Mithon. A copy of a royal grant of nobility of 1776 permitting the bearing of new arms to be settled by the Juge d'Armes is in Nouveau d'Hozier 289,

Dossier 6682. An analogous document is printed in Dessalles and Frémont (1974), 124-125.

(10)   Nisbet (1722-1742) I, 98; Stevenson (1914), 81, 121, 269-271; Grant (1945), Introduction; Innes and Innes (1978), 6, Plate IV; Flynn (1978), 9-10.

(11)   Fauchet (1606), 22, 27vo, 28; Nisbet (1722-1742) II, Part IV, 172; Vulson de La Colombière (1838), 403-406, 439; Du Roure de Paulin (1906), 11; Wagner (1956), 11, 56-60, 161.

(12)   Le Feron (1555), 28vo., 43vo.; Fauchet (1606), 22, 28; Favyn (1620) I, 56, 58; Dupuy Demportes (1754) II, 365; Vulson de La Colombière (1838), 403-406, 424-425, 439; Du Roure de Paulin (1906), 11-12; Mathieu (1946), 186; Wagner (1956), 9-11, 56-58, 73-77; (1967), 29.

(13)   Cadot (1697), 57; Cherin (1788), 92-93, 289; Grandmaison (1904-1905) I, 9-10; Mathieu (1946), 71; Grolée-Virville (1978), 19. There was a hiatus in the office of Juge d'Armes from 1696 to 1701, but the former Juge d'Armes, as Keeper of the Armorial Général, issued certificates of registration which had the effect of grants of arms; moreover, by virtue of an Order in Council of 1696 he continued to settle the arms of newly ennobled persons.

(14)   Cherin (1788), 289; Grandmaison (1904-1905) II, 49; Mathieu (1946), 72; Meurgey de Tupigny (1965-1967) I, xx; Dessalles and Frémont (1974), 126; Grolée-Virville (1978), 39-40; Nouveau d'Hozier 289, Dossier 6682.

(15)   Du Boscq de Beaumont (1906), 165-166; Mathieu (1946), 72.

(16)   Grandmaison (1904-1905) II, 89-90; Du Boscq de Beaumont (1906), 166-169, 174; Mathieu (1946), 71-72; Grolée-Virville (1978), Plates XXI, XXIII. It seems that after the Revolution the archives of the Juge d'Armes contained the drafts of about 3000 settlements of arms made between 1701 and 1789 (Grolée-Virville (1978), 210).

(17)   X (1900), 100-104; Hope and Wagner (1953), 67-69; Wagner (1956), 59-63, 77, 89, 136-137, 162; (1967), 39, 67-68, 126-127, 145; (1978), 30; Squibb (1985), 68-71.

(18)   Wagner (1956), 79, 90, 96-99.

(19)   Wagner (1956), 9-10, 81, 98-99; (1967), 179-180, 202; Squibb (1985), 73-74, 130.

(20)   Wagner (1967), 294; Squibb (1985), 125-126.

(21)   Observations (1724), 49; Edmondson (1780) I, 146; Howard (1866-1902), passim; Baildon (1904) (July), 52-54, 57-60; Bannerman (1904-1916), passim; Stevenson (1914), 86; Clarke (1916-1938), passim; Fox-Davies (1949), 589; Squibb (1956), 33; (1959), 140; (1985), 60-63, 104-105, 123-126; Wagner (1967), 187, 294; Dennys (1982) 137-138.

(22)   Squibb (1956), 57-58.

(23)   Nichols (1863), 465-466; X (1900), 104-108; Fox-Davies (1949), 589; Full Report (1955), 55, 56; P (1955), 147; Squibb (1956), 58; (1981) 448, 477; (1985), 71-73, 75-77; Dennys (1982), 156-157. For the modern procedure leading to a grant of arms in England, see Dennys (1982), 156-157.

(24)   Seton (1863), 72-73; Grant (1945), Introduction.

(25)   Act (1672); Mackenzie (1680), 8; Seton (1863), 57, 285, 490-492; Stevenson (1914), 451-455; Bruce (1980), 16.

(26)   Mackenzie (1680), 8; Seton (1863), 28-31; Act (1867); Stevenson (1914), 39-41, 46, 81, 86-87, 453-455; (1926), 1; Heraldica (1940), 131; Innes and Innes (1978), 4-7, 9, 45, 123. For the modern procedure leading to a grant of arms in Scotland, see Innes and Innes (1978), 46-48.

(27)   Seton (1863), 21, and Stevenson (1914), 72-73 (both citing the case of M'Donnell v. Macdonald in 1826); Stevenson (1926), 8; Innes (1930), 335, 342; Heraldica (1940), 131; Fox-Davies (1949), 589; Innes and Innes (1978), 8-9, 46, 51, 52; Dennys (1982), 156.

Chapter 6 – Assumed Arms

(1)   Mackenzie (1680), 12; La Roque (1734), Noblesse, 89-91; Mathieu (1946), 136, 154; Squibb (1959), 180-181; (1967), 6-7.

(2)   La Roque (1734), Noblesse, 91; Pastoret (1811-1840) XVII, 98-99; XVIII, 58-59, 192-193; XIX, 556-558; Mathieu (1946), 185, 188 (Note 1). In a Royal Ordinance of 1467 on the trades and corporations of Paris it was stated that each was to have a banner with a white cross and "such ensigns and arms as the said trades and companies shall decide" (Pastoret (1811-1840), XVI, 673).

(3)   La Roque (1734), Noblesse, 223; Noms, 48, 50; Prinet (1917), 147-154; Mathieu (1946), 47-48, 187.

(4)	Cherin (1788), 288-289; Mathieu (1946), 72; Meurgey de Tupigny (1965-1967) I, xx.

(5)   Hallez d'Arros (1891), 28; Tesson (1897), 15-17; Mathieu (1946), 87; Du Puy de Clinchamps (1978), 51.

(6)   Mathieu (1946), 137-142, 165-166.

(7)   Sailly (1870), 174-176; Chamillart (1887-1888) II, 754 (Note); Chambois and Farcy (1895), 143-145; Prevost (1910) I, 266; II, 130, 137, 156, 158; (1922-1924) I, 16, 21, 61, 136, 148, 151; II, 8, 10, 20, 43, 105, 106, 108; Jougla (1934-1952) II, 272; Mathieu (1946), 140-142, 165-166.

(8)   Mackenzie (1680), 12; Innes (1940E), 206. It has been suggested that, by a legal fiction, "every right to arms is held to flow from a grant" (Stevenson (1914), 333; Innes and Innes (1978), 45); this does not seem to be universally accepted as a principle (Innes (1941A), 131, Note 32; Moncreiffe (1982), 13).

(9)   Act (1592); Act (1672); Innes (1929), 561; (1930), 335, 341; Innes and Innes (1978), 45.

(10)   For samples of the arguments for and against the "second type" of prescription, see (a) for: Barron (1902) (July), 40-47; Baildon (1904); Round (1907), xix-xxiii; Pine (1963), 72-74, 90-91, 126,137; and (b) against: Phillimore (1903A); (1903B); Fox-Davies (1949), 21-23; Squibb (1959), 178-189; (1967), 2-3, 5-15; Brooke-Little (1969), Note 2; (1978), 13, 264-265; Dennys (1982), 152-156. Some of the arguments are summarised in Wagner (1967), 541-546. Specific points in the arguments of both sides are developed in a number of articles and letters in The Coat of Arms in Volume III in 1954-1955 and in New Series, Volumes I - III in 1975-1978; specific references are No.17, 30-32; No.18, 43-44, 62; No.19, 109-111, 114; No.21, 206; No.22, 248-249; No.23, 290-291; No.96, 252-253; No.101, 143-144; No.107, 83-84. It is not always clear what sense a writer gives to "prescription". Thus, while it seems to be Baildon's view that a few generations is enough to give title to arms, he seems to be saying in one place (Baildon (1904) (January), 124) that it is necessary to be able to presume use since before the limit of legal memory.

(11)   X (1900), 44, 45; Wagner (1956), 63-64, 73, 125; Squibb (1959), 181-182.

(12)   Wagner (1956), 9-10; Squibb (1985), 128-132.

(13)   Squibb (1956), 59, 79-80, 93; (1959), 183-185; (1967), 9-11; (1981), 476. In what appears to be the last recorded case in the Court of Chivalry before its revival in 1954, a defendant produced a pedigree going back to the late sixteenth century and, without reference to any grant of arms or Visitation entry, claimed a right to bear arms ex prescriptione et jure antecessorio (Squibb (1956), 113-115). No decision is recorded.

(14)   Barron (1902) (July), 43-45; Baildon (1904) (January), 141-142; Wagner (1956), 3. As late as 1714 the Kings of Arms confirmed arms to a man on the strength of use by his grandfather (Baildon (1904) (July), 63; cf. Squibb (1985), 121).

(15)   According to the Cambridge Armorial (1985), 66, the arms of St. Catharine's College, Cambridge, were recorded at the Visitation of 1684 as having been anciently borne and used by the college. As the college was founded in 1473, there was no question of its having borne the arms since time immemorial.

(16)   P (1955), 147; Full Report (1955), 57.

(17)   X (1900), 139; Baildon (1904), (July), 65-66; Squibb (1959), 187-189, (1967), 14-15; Brooke-Little (1978), 13, 264-265; Dennys (1982), 153-155. It seems that an exception to the rule of practice may be made if the period of use is proved to extend back to before 1673. That was the first year for which almost full records of grants of arms exist, so that arms used since before that year could be the subject of an early grant of which no record remains, and this appears to be the basis on which such an exception may be made (Squibb, op.cit.).

Chapter 7 - Transmission

(1)   Howard (1890), 72-73.

(2)   FMN (1865), 12-15; Butcher (1926), 345-352, 358-359.

(3)   Fox-Davies (1949), 478.

(4)   After the death of Sir John Knightley late in the fourteenth century his daughter brought lands and the arms of Knightley to her husband Roger Peshall; this couple's daughter, Joan Peshall inherited the lands and the shield of Knightley (Barron (1902) (April), 4). The arms of Wellesborough were assigned by the last heir male of the family to someone who seems to have purchased his lands and/or to have married his daughter and heiress; it is therefore uncertain whether the assignment was an adjunct to a sale of the land or merely a confirmation of the husband's right to use his wife's inherited arms (Littledale (1926), 223-224). The attempt by an inhabitant of Berwick

to bequeath his arms to his son-in-law by his will of 1568 may be considered to be somewhat analogous; this attempt may be said to have succeeded, since the arms bequeathed, or very similar arms, appear to have been confirmed to the son-in-law by Garter (Littledale (1926), 222-223). The modern view is that all such transmissions would require a Royal Licence in order to be effective.

(5)   Dallaway (1793), 372; Doubleday (1916), 651-753; Heraldica (1940), 76-77; Innes (1940D), 365; (1941A), 129; Fox-Davies (1949), 526, 542, 543, 546-547; Squibb (1956), 58; (1981), 446, 457; Brooke-Little (1978), 131, 140, 145, 147; Dennys (1982), 13. It appears that until the sixteenth century an English heiress could transmit her arms entire to her heir even if her own husband had no arms (see, for example, Innes of Learney (Sir T.), The Armorial House or Family, in Notes and Queries CLXXVII (1939) (September), 167).

(6)   Mackenzie (1680), 70-71; Seton (1863), 321-357; Stevenson (1914), 335-354; Innes (1941B), 2-4; Innes and Innes (1978), Preface, 68.

(7)   Cf. Mackenzie (1680), 75.

(8)   Innes (1938A), 97; (1940A), 294, 297; (1940B), 309-311; (1940C), 362-365; (1941A), 129; (1941B) 2-4; Heraldica (1940), 76-77, 93-94, 95-96; (1942), 92-94.

(9)   Stevenson (1914), 356; Innes (1940A), 272, 294; (1940B), 308-309; (1940C), 362-365; Heraldica (1940)432; (1942), 94; Innes and Innes (1978), 63.

(10)   Mackenzie (1680), 80-81; Innes (1938A), 97; (1940B), 308-310; (1940C), 362-364; (1940D), 364; (1941B), 3; Heraldica (1940), 94, 132; Innes and Innes (1978), 81. In a nineteenth century instance in which the Lord Lyon indicated that it would be preferable for a son to bear his mother's arms alone, his father was in fact armigerous, but it is clear that the same view would have been taken by the Lord Lyon if the father had had no arms of his own (Innes (1940B), 308-310, especially the second column on page 309).

(11)   It may be worthwhile to consider in greater detail the case in which the heir to Scottish arms is the eldest of a number of sisters. If she marries and enters her husband's family so that she and her issue take his name, then her issue may either bear her husband's arms alone or quarter the two arms, the husband's arms being in the principal quarters. The entering into her husband's family causes the heiress to become "conventionally dead", and her rights as heir to the unquartered arms may be taken by her next sister. And so on with each sister in turn. If all the sisters become "conventionally dead",

then the right to bear the whole arms passes to the next heir. If on the other hand the eldest sister's issue remains in her family by taking her name, and so being entitled to bear her arms, these may be borne alone (which is preferable) or quartered with the husband's arms if he has arms (the latter being placed in subordinate quarters). As for the younger sisters, as junior co-heirs they may transmit their arms to their issue as subordinate quarterings in shields in which their respective husbands' arms form the principal quarterings. If any of these younger sisters (junior co-heirs) wishes her issue to bear arms based on her paternal arms (either as their only arms or as the principal quarterings in shields also containing her husband's arms), this is possible if her issue takes her name and if a duly differenced version of her paternal arms is matriculated; such a junior co-heir is then in an armorial situation analogous to that of a younger son, and is herself a cadet of her family. Any possible confusion or duplication in the operation of these various processes is avoided by the requirement for matriculation in all of them, whereby the Lord Lyon's approval and confirmation are required to give effect to these processes.

(12)   Mackenzie (1680), 81; Innes (1929), 558; (1940D), 362; Innes and Innes (1978), 76.

(13)   By an independant branch of a family is meant one which subsists well away from other branches, for example in a different part of the country, or abroad. A number of examples of transmissions of arms through women are mentioned in La Roque (1734), Noblesse, 16, 34; Noms, 36-41, 47, 51-53; Mathieu (1946), 143-152. Many other examples can be found in published collections of genealogies of French noble families. Taking just one of these, Rivoire de La Batie (1867), we note the following armorial transfers in the province of Dauphiny in which a woman was the link between the two families concerned (page references are in parentheses): seven in the sixteenth century: Adhémar-Castellane (3, 125), Blain-Marcel (78, 379-380), Césarges-Meffrey (126, 401-402), Coct-Monteynard (162, 433), Gadagne-Hostun (248, 311-312), La Tour-Meugnier (408, 739), Vesc-Agoult (785-786), five in the seventeenth century: Béatrix-Robert-Moret (56, 98, 447), Grolée-Du Cros (181, 290), Soliers-Guette (297, 707), Tertulle-La Baume (55), Thiennes-Musy (463, 727-728); and six in the eighteenth century: Arvillars-Luzy (23, 368), Grolée-Olivier (292, 478-479), La Balme-Lombard (36-37, 358-359), Louvet-Merlin (365, 407), Solignac-Du Vivier (708, 812), Thiennes (Musy)-Novel (473-474, 727-728); in almost all instances the name was also taken.

(14)   La Roque (1734), Noms, 37-41, 52; Mathieu (1946), 148.

(15)   La Roque (1734), Noblesse, 16; Noms, 36, 37; Mathieu (1946), 147, 150.

(16)   La Roque (1734), Noms, 37, 41; Prinet (1909), 379; Mathieu (1946), 144, 150-151.

(17)   Mathieu (1946), 142-143, 148.

(18)   Brillon (1711) II, 792; La Roque (1734), Noblesse, 140; Ferrières and Boucher d'Argis (1787) II, 284; Innes (1940A), 296; Mathieu (1946), 127-128; Du Puy de Clinchamps (1978), 35-36. There were other parts of France in which, in the absence of sons, eldest daughters of noble families had certain advantageous rights of inheritance to property; cf. La Roque (1734), Noblesse, 112; Bacquet (1744), 347; Meyer (1972), 65.

(19)   La Roque (1734), Noblesse, 223; Noms, 48, 50; Prinet (1917), 147-154; Mathieu (1946), 146-147, 194-195. An example of those who thought that the 1556 law was and remained a general law is Ferrières and Boucher d'Argis (1787) I, 286. La Roque seems to have taken a similar view.

(20)   La Roque (1734), Noms, 50; Mathieu (1946), 151-153, 272-274.

(21)   Joan Peshall, who inherited the arms of Knightley as mentioned in Note 4, married but had no children; in 1436 she conveyed her shield of Knightley to her paternal cousin Richard Peshall, excluding herself and all others of her (married) name from any right therein; this conveyance of the arms was followed by a conveyance of the lands of Knightley to the same Richard Peshall. In another instance in the early fifteenth century, a sale of land was accompanied by an assignment of arms said to have been borne by the tenants of the land since the Conquest (Littledale (1926), 220-221). Examples where no land is mentioned include Morley (1348/9), Beaumeys (1391), and Clanvowe (1410) (Edmondson (1780) I, 156; Littledale (1926), 219, 223; Wagner (1956), 20).

(22)   Rylands (1911), 134, 183-184.

(23)   Some examples of Royal Licences between 1790 and 1920 authorising the taking up of name and arms by a husband or relation are in Marshall (1877), 116, 278; (1882), 33, 34; (1883), 23, 270; Harwood (1916), 116, 117. An example of an early, eighteenth century Royal Licence authorising the taking up of name and arms by the legatee of certain property is printed in Littledale (1926), 134. For the procedure involved, see Nichols (1863), 11; Squibb (1981), 477, 478.

(24)   Round (1907), 94, 466; Gibbs (1913), 589-591; Squibb (1981), 460.

(25)   Mackenzie (1680), 70-71; Nichols (1867), 82; Gibbs (1913), 589; Stevenson (1914), 355-363; Innes (1933), 188; (1940A), 254-257, 273-275, 293-297; (1941B), 2-3; Heraldica (1940), 75, 93-94, 95, 133; (1942), 98; Innes and Innes (1978), 57, 61, 65-60; Squibb (1981), 460.

(26)   If the holder of the arms makes a nomination within the terms of the then existing matriculation (for example if the latter gives the destination of the arms as "descendants" and if the holder nominates a descendant other than the heir), then it is normally a straightforward matter to obtain a rematriculation giving effect to the nomination (cf. Adam (F.), The Clans, Septs and Regiments of the Scottish Highlands, Eighth Edition, revised by Sir T. Innes of Learney (1970), 174-175, 613).

(27)   La Roque (1734), Noms, 55; Mathieu (1946), 164-165.

(28)   Brillon (1711) I, 823; La Roque (1734), Noms, 39-40; Mathieu (1946), 113, 143-153; D'Haucourt and Durivault (1965), 37. Such was the importance attached to family that dispositions of name and arms in favour of wholly unrelated persons, never very common, became rarer in later times. Even when the disponee was in no way descended from the family whose name and arms he was to receive, some blood relationship between him and the disponer can often be found. Although François de Vachon, who assumed the name and arms of Briançon in the eighteenth century in accordance with the terms of the will of Nicolas de Briançon (last of the family), does not seem to have had any Briançon blood, François was the nephew of Marie de Vachon who was the mother of Nicolas de Briançon, so that François and Nicolas were first cousins (Rivoire de La Batie (1867), 109-110,758-759).

(29)   Brillon (1711) I, 155; Mathieu (1946), 143-145.

(30)   Brillon (1711) I, 155,823; La Roque (1734), Noms, 48, 50; Borel d'Hauterive (1849-1850), 346-347; Prinet (1917), 147-154; Mathieu (1946), 145-146.

(31)   Brillon (1711) II, 793.

(32)   Innes (1941A), 129; Mathieu (1946), 190; Fox-Davies (1949), 347-348; Galbreath and Jéquier (1977), 246-249; Innes and Innes (1978), 51. An example of English medieval practice, where a man used the arms of his father in law, had both those arms and his father's arms on his tomb, and transmitted the latter to his son, is in Norton

(1982), 18. Numerous instances of French families having two arms are to be found in, for example, Jougla (1934-1952).

(33)   Fox-Davies (1949), 347; Brooke-Little (1969), Note 172; (1978), Plate XXVIII. According to a manuscript which may be attributable to Glover, the sixteenth century antiquary, "there is no man of any degree that beareth more than one only arms, which is properly his own" (Dallaway (1793), 369). The notion that the Kings of Arms could wholly extinguish existing lawful arms seems a questionable one, as the English Kings of Arms now appreciate (Brooke-Little (1969), Note 172). The French Juge d'Armes believed he could issue a settlement of arms cancelling an earlier settlement and replacing the arms (Grandmaison (1904-1905) I, 60-62). Settlements of arms did not have the legal status of grants, and were perhaps more easily revocable.

Chapter 8 - Differencing

(1)   The use of various methods of differencing at various periods and in various families of the three countries is exemplified in Anselme (1726-1733) III, 551-656; Nisbet (1722-1742) I; Dallaway (1793), Plate VII; Dugdale (1811), 11-13; Woodward and Burnett (1892), 402-452; Stevenson (1914) Plate XXXVII; Johnston (G.H.) The Heraldry of the Campbells (1920, reprinted 1977); Adam-Even (1949), 115-120; Gayre (1961), 28-92; Galbreath and Jéquier (1977), 145; La Force (1972).

(2)   The label, widely used as a brisure from early times, was rarely used as an ordinary charge after the fourteenth century, although there are instances of its use as such in new French arms until at least the seventeenth century. For example, the arms of Pierre Antoine de Micoud, ennobled in 1654, were: gules, a bend argent charged in chief with a label sable.

(3)   Seton (1863), 195-198; Stevenson (1914), 279-310; Prinet (1932), 4-6, 10-11; Collins (1946); Mathieu (1946), 99-103; Adam-Even (1949), 15-16; (1961-1968); Hope and Wagner (1953), 56-61; Gayre (1961), 38-39, 45-51, 54-63; Galbreath and Jéquier (1977), 145, 235-238; Dennys (1982), 18, 105.

(4)   Favyn (1620) I, 18-19; Menestrier (1696), 216-226; Woodward and Burnett (1892), 413-425; Fox-Davies (1949), 479-481. In English heraldry it was at one time possible to use a label as the permanent difference of the line of an heir male when the whole arms had passed through a female heir of line, as in the Hastings arms which were the subject of the Grey v. Hastings case (Guillim (1666), 33). In Scottish heraldry a label can be used for the same purpose, or as the

permanent difference of the line of an "heir" from whom the whole arms have been diverted (Innes (1940A), 274, 295; Innes and Innes (1978), 65).

(5)   Woodward and Burnett (1892), 437-444; Fox-Davies (1949), 481, 500-503; Innes and Innes (1978), 54-55; Dennys (1982), 18, 105-106.

(6)   Woodward and Burnett (1892), 430-431.

(7)   Collins (1946), 173; Galbreath and Jéquier (1977), 237.

(8)   Favyn (1620) I, 18-19; Guillim (1666), 37; Mackenzie (1680), 72-73; Nisbet (1722-1742) II, Part III, 14-17; Edmondson (1780) I, 168; Dallaway (1793), 381-382; Woodward and Burnett (1892) 444-446; Stevenson (1914), 280-281; Littledale (1926), 40, 135-136; Fox-Davies (1949), 487-490; Gayre (1961), 128-130; Galbreath and Jéquier (1977), 250; Innes and Innes (1978), 54-55; Dennys (1982), 19.

(9)   While the dates at which individual parts of the "Ordinances of the Duke of Clarence" were formulated are somewhat uncertain, it appears that all these Ordinances were accepted as governing the activities of the Kings of Arms towards the end of the fifteenth century. A clause in the oath taken by the provincial Kings of Arms during that century required them to record the "noble gentlemen" of their province "and such arms as they bear with the differences due in arms to be given". Cf. Wagner (1956), 59, 137.

(10)   Dallaway (1793), 369-370.

(11)   Dugdale (1811), 23-32.

(12)   Dugdale (1811), 25; Seton (1863), 86; Baildon (1904) (July), 59; Wagner (1956), 148.

(13)   Bannerman (1904), 296-299; Littledale (1925) 44-45.

(14)   Ruvigny (1904), 195, 197, 201.

(15)   Howard (1866-1902), passim; Bannerman (1904-1916), passim; Clarke (1916-1938), passim; Littledale (1925), passim; (1926), passim. Of about 150 grants and confirmations of the sixteenth century published in these works, about two fifths stipulated that the descendants were to bear the arms with differences; of about 200 grants and confirmations of the seventeenth, eighteenth and nineteenth centuries, about three quarters contained this stipulation.

(16)   Squibb (1956), 84-86.

(17)   Dallaway (1793), 381; Woodward and Burnett (1892), 397; Brooke-Little (1978), 116-118.

(18)   X (1900), 113-115; Clarke (1920-1922), 155, 178-179, 191; Fox-Davies (1949), 345, 489; Squibb (1959), 189; (1981), 445; Brooke-Little (1978), Plate XXVIII; Dennys (1982), 19.

(19)   Full Report (1955), 54.

(20)   Fox-Davies (1949), 492; Brooke-Little (1978), 118.

(21)   Scohier (1597), 21-25, 69; Favyn (1620) I, 18-19; Expilly (1636), 712; Segoing (1657), 457-459; Geliot and Palliot (1661), 100, 107-115; Menestrier (1696), 216-226; Brillon (1711) I, 155; La Roche-Flavin and Graverol (1745), 635; Dupuy Demportes (1754) I, 91-92, 95; Mathieu (1946), 99-114.

(22)   Mathieu (1946), 102.

(23)   Mathieu (1946), 127.

(24)   Scohier (1597), 30-33, 68-70; Favyn (1620) I, 18-19; Varennes (1640), 517-535; Segoing (1657), 459; Geliot and Palliot (1661), 100, 107; Menestrier (1696), 216-226; Dupuy Demportes (1754) I, 92-94.

(25)   Mathieu (1946), 68, 99-104.

(26)   Mathieu (1946), 106.

(27)   Brillon (1711) I, 155; La Roche-Flavin and Graverol (1745), 635.

(28)   Mathieu (1946), 105-106, 110-111. It has been pointed out that this case shows how the medieval nexus between arms and fief (land) had become loosened (Mathieu (1946), 106).

(29)   The report of the Salvaing case appears in Expilly (1636), 709-711. There are references to the case in Varennes (1640), 157-158; Mackenzie (1680), 71. (cited in Innes (1940A), 273) and in Mathieu (1946), 104, 180. That the case was a hoax is shown in Terrebasse (1850), 171-176.

(30)   Cherin (1788), 91-93; Grolée-Virville (1978), 18.

(31)   Menestrier (1696), 216-226; Brillon (1711) I, 155; Dupuy Demportes (1754) I, 95; Ferrières and Boucher d'Argis (1787) I, 123; Cherin (1788), 245-250; Mathieu (1946), 102-104, 109. The practice of

differencing survived to some extent in the Royal Family and in some great families. Traces of the practice are occasionally found in other families. Examples may be found in the Marcé and perhaps the Prevost families of the region of Tours (Chambois and Farcy (1895), 494-495, 615-617). The general abandonment of the practice is illustrated by the arms registered in the Armorial Général of 1696-1709; the various members of each family usually gave in the same arms, and the officials, intent only on maximizing the financial yield, made no attempt to difference them. Eventually the sons and grandsons of the King himself were permitted to use the undifferenced royal arms of France (Pinoteau (1976), xxiv, xxvi-xxvii, xxxvii and publications there cited). Nevertheless, some writers continued to insist that the differencing of the arms of cadets was obligatory, even after the final abolition of the monarchy (for example, Maigne (W), Abrégé méthodique de la Science des Armoiries (1860), 122).

(32)   Woodward and Burnett (1892), 397-398.

(33)   Seton (1863), 130-131; Howard (1874), 356; (1884), 179, 189, 259; X (1900), 165-171; Stevenson (1914), 126; Clarke (1916-1917), 254-256; Littledale (1925), 33-34; 79-80, 82-83; Heraldica (1940), 75; Fox-Davies (1949), 500.

(34)   Act (1592); Act (1672); Nichols (1865), 397-398, 404; Paul (1903), xi-xii; Stevenson (1914), 464, 466; Clarke (1916-1917), 254-256; Fox-Davies (1949), 500; Innes and Innes (1978), 49, 54-60.

(35)   X (1900), 168-171; Innes (1940A), 297; Fox-Davies (1949), 500-503; Innes and Innes (1978), 51, 54-62.

(36)   Stevenson (1914), 281-282; Heraldica (1940), 77; 132; Innes and Innes (1978), 50, 53, 58, 66, 69, 75, 79, 80, 81. Cf. The Complete Peerage, revised edition VIII (1932), 475, note f.

(37)   Woodward and Burnett (1892), 419; Innes (1938A), 97; Innes and Innes (1978), 50, 65 (and see the Second Edition (1956), Plate XXIX). The eldest son of the heir may use the arms with a label of five points, which he may replace with his father's label of three points if his father dies before succeeding to the whole arms (Innes 1938A), 97; Innes and Innes (1978), 50, 65). There is a somewhat analogous practice in English heraldry (Fox-Davies (1949), 487).

(38)   Nichols (1865), 399-400, 404; Stevenson (1914), 70-71, 350, 466-467; Innes (1940A), 295; Gayre and Gayre (1964-1969) I, 115; Innes and Innes (1978), 60. In 1795 the Lyon Depute declared that a Patent of the arms of the chief of Clan Cameron given in 1792 to Cameron of

Erracht was void because he had obtained it by misrepresenting himself as the representative of the family; the arms were declared to be those of Cameron of Lochiel, the true chief of Clan Cameron (Stewart (1974), 147, 303-304).

(39)   Mackenzie (1680), 75; Menestrier (1696), 218; Dupuy Demportes (1754) I, 97; Seton (1863), 96, 101-116; Woodward and Burnett (1892), 446-447; Mathieu (1946), 100 (Note); Fox-Davies (1949), 483, 489; Galbreath and Jéquier (1977), 237; Innes and Innes (1978), 76, 82; Brooke-Little (1978), 118.

(40)   Woodward and Burnett (1892), 548-572; Gayre (1961), 100-111.

(41)   Nisbet (1722-1742) II, 26, 28; Woodward and Burnett (1892), 562-565; Brooke-Little (1969), Note 236; (1978), 123,124; Dennys (1982), 19-20.

(42)   Woodward and Burnett (1892), 565-569; Heraldica (1940), 77; Innes and Innes (1978), 60-62, 81; Brooke-Little (1978), 123.

(43)   Woodward and Burnett (1892), 569; Brooke-Little (1978), 123; Innes and Innes (1978), 56.

(44)   Expilly (1636), 712; La Roque (1734), Noblesse, 121; Ferrières and Boucher d'Argis (1787) I, 286; Cherin (1788), 83, 235-236; Woodward and Burnett (1892), 551-553, 570-572; Mathieu (1946), 127-123; Galbreath and Jéquier (1977), 122.

(45)   Brooke-Little (1969), Note 236; (1978), 124; Dennys (1982), 20.

(46)   Innes and Innes. (1978), 67, 70 (and see the Second Edition (1956), 100); Brooke-Little (1969), Note 236.

(47)   Mathieu (1946), 98, 113, 152.

Chapter 9 - Surveys

(1)   Maugard (1788), 83, 202-203; Vulson de La Colombière (1838), 403-404, 439; Du Roure de Paulin (1906), 11; Wagner (1956), 11, 56-63, 88, 90, 93, 106-118, 136-137, 161; (1967), 34, 132, 137; Adam-Even (1957), 30-31; D'Haucourt and Durivault (1965), 30; Squibb (1985), 128-129.

(2)   Observations (1724), 50-52; Dallaway (1793), 310; Seton (1863), 177-178; Markland (1865), 151-154; X (1900), 120-125; Armytage (1910), viii; Rylands (1911), v; Wagner (1956), 9-10, 118-119, 139-143; (1967), 161; Squibb (1981), 447-448; (1985), 130-141.

(3)   Full Report (1955), 49.

(4)   Observations (1724), 51-52; Edmondson (1780) I, 160; Dallaway
        (1793), 313-314; X (1900), 125-129, 133-134; Baildon (1904)
        (January), 117; Rylands (1911), 151-152; Rylands and Bannerman
        (1922), 36-37, Squibb (1956), 1-5; (1985), 140-144; Wagner (1956), 3-
        4, 149; (1967), 187, 267-273.

(5)   Vulson de La Colombière (1838), 406; Contamine (1976), 31.

(6)   Cadot (1697), 41-152; Maugard (1788), 90-91; Cherin (1788), 220-223,
        227-228; Hallez d'Arros, (1891), 19-32; Tesson (1897), 1-19, 185; Du
        Boscq de Beaumont (1906), 175-176; Prevost (1910), vii-lii; Mathieu
        (1946), 75-87; Meurgey de Tupigny (1965-1967) I, vii-xli; Le Second
        Ordre (1973), 232-236; Du Puy de Clinchamps (1978), 50-51; Grolée-
        Virville (1978), 38-39, 107-126, Plates XVII-XIX.

(7)   Cadot (1697), 160; Mathieu (1946), 208.

(8)   Boulaud (1910), 197-217; Meurgey de Tupigny (1965-1967) I, xv. See
        also the case of the Brossard family, mentioned in Chapter 6.

(9)   Examples of printed portions of the Armorial Général relating to
        certain provinces or portions thereof are in Montgrand (1864);
        Bouchot (1875); Dufau de Maluquer (1889); Moreau de Pravieux
        (1894); Gosset (1903); Prevost (1910); (1913); (1922-1924); Chassin
        du Guerny (1930); Meurgey de Tupigny (1965-1967). References to
        other printed extracts will be found in Le Second Ordre (1973), 236.

(10)   D'Hozier (1738-1768); Grolée-Virville (1978), 141-163, 173.

(11)   Cherin (1788), 374-376; Maugard (1788), 109-110, 114,194; La
        Villegille (1856), 361; Marion (1923), 25; Mathieu (1946), 49, 87-89;
        Meurgey de Tupigny (1965-1967) I, xx-xxiv; Durye (1974), 11;
        Grolée-Virville (1978), 127-128. Cherin and, following him, Mathieu
        and Meurgey de Tupigny state simply that the Parlement condemned
        the Ordinance of 1760 as being contrary to the usages of the
        Kingdom, so that it was never applied. According to La Villegille, the
        Ordinance was withdrawn on 30 August 1760 by the King, who
        replaced it with an Edict which was sent to the Parlement. No such
        Edict is mentioned by Cherin in his collection of statutes published in
        1788. Whatever the sequence of events, it is clear that the contents of
        the 1760 Ordinance failed to become law.

(12)   Observations (1724), 50-52; Edmondson (1780) I, 158-160; Dallaway
        (1793), 309-315; Markland (1865), 151-154; CHA (1879), 206-208; X

(1900), 120-134; Baildon (1904) (January), 117; Armytage (1910), vii-x; Rylands (1911), v, 151-152; Rylands and Bannerman (1922), 36-37; Wagner (1956), 3-4, 9, 58-60, 136-137, 149; (1967), 161, 185-187, 267-268; (1978), 34-35; Squibb (1959), 35; (1978); (1981), 447; (1985), 128-144.

(13)   Squibb (1959), 212. In the sixteenth century the Earl Marshal claimed he could fine anyone who offended after having disclaimed (Wagner (1967), 186); it is not clear whether a formal sentence of the Court of Chivalry was necessary.

(14)   Dallaway (1793), 163-167; Wagner (1956), 4, 105, 147; (1967), 205-208, 268-269; (1978), 78. Many of the Visitation records have been published by local record or antiquarian societies, others by the Harleian Society; the material published does not always correspond to the originals (Squibb (1978); (1981), 448).

(15)   Some of the recorded material has been published, for example in Bouton (1863-1877) I, 146-149, 216-219, 287-288, 367-370, 407-413, 423-431; Tesson (1899), 1-132; Durand de Saint-Front (1968), 187-216, 239-276.

(16)   Cherin (1788), 104-105.

(17)   La Roque (1734), Noblesse, 418-421; Cherin (1788), 120, 122-123, 126-131, 134-140, 145-147.

(18)   Brillon (1711) II, 792; La Roque (1734), Noblesse, 407-411, 422-426; D'Hozier (1738-1768), Register I, Second Part, 684, 685, 688, 693-694, 696; Cherin (1788), xxxi, li, 148-157, 162-168, 172-179, 187-190, 193, 215, 217, 219-220, 226-227, 230-231, 236, 238-250, 252-253, 256, 260-268, 282-283, 286-287, 298-299, 309-314, 323-324, 328-329, 331-338, 341, 348, 354-355, 357-359; Maugard (1788), 44, 70-71, 109-110, 114-115, 119-120, 169; Chamillart (1887-1889) I, vi-x, 3-7; Chambois and Farcy (1895), vi, 1-2; Tesson (1899), 18; Meyer (1972), 44-55; Grolée-Virville (1978), 36-37.

(19)   D'Hozier (1738-1768), Register I, Second Part, 698-701; Cherin (1788), xxxii-xxxiii, 168, 173, 175-176, 187, 217, 239-241, 244-250, 255, 262, 264, 268, 310-311, 331-332, 425; Chamillart (1887-1889) I, xii; Supplement, 60. Strictly speaking, the Declaration of 1714 applied only to families which could not be proved to have been non-noble before the beginning of the qualifying century.

(20)   Maugard (1788), 70-71, 114-115; Belleguise (1923) I, ix-x; Chamiliart (1887-1889) II, 765-816. There were omissions in the English Visitations too (cf. Squibb (1978), 5-6).

(21)   Cherin (1788), 193, 242-243, 354-355; Maugard (1788), 91; Durye (1974), 14.

(22)   Examples of printed portions of the records of the Nobiliary Survey of 1666 etc. (often including the arms of the families) are in Lefevre de Caumartin (1673); Des Diguères (1865); Melleville (1867); Chamillart (1887-1889); Cumont (1890); La Bouralière (1892-1893); Chambois and Farcy (1895); Toulgouet-Treanna (1901); Ribier (1907-1912); Belleguise (1923).

(23)   Act (1592); Nisbet (1722-1742) II, Part IV, 172; Seton (1863), 175-176; Stevenson (1914), 83; Innes and Innes (1978), 43-44; Bruce (1980), 14. While there seems to be no record of any general Visitation, heralds have sometimes been sent by Lyon to "visit" particular displays of arms (e.g., Innes (1930), 343).

(24)   Act (1672); Innes (1930), 340; Innes and Innes (1978), 43-44.

(25)   Seton (1863), 175-176.

(26)   Paul (1903); Gayre and Gayre (1964-1969); Reid and Wilson (1977).

(27)   Cameron and Polaczek (1938), 51-74; Lart (1938), 76-88, 150-155; Innes (1930), 335; (1940E), 201; (1946), 126-128; Grant (1945), Introduction; Innes and Innes (1978), 96-100, Plate III.

(28)   Howard (1880), 298; (1886), 99, 324; (1888), Frontispiece; (1900), 261; Bannerman (1906), 41-42; (1914), 1-2; Clarke (1916-1917), 130, 171-180, 217-218; (1918-1919), 234; (1926-1928), 1-2; (1935-1937), 210; (1938), 11-12; Littledale (1925), 4, 7, 29-30, 32, 52-53, 59-61, 63-64, 66-67, 71-72, 85-86, 108-109, 122-123; (1926), 135, 138-140, 147-149, 151-156, 159, 161, 167-168, 177, 179-181, 190-194; Lart (1938), 177-179, 182; Squibb (1956), 28-29; Wagner (1967), 316, 418-419; Arundel de Condé (1981), 169.

(29)   Cherin (1788), 357-359.

(30)   D'Hozier (1738-1768), Register I, Second Part, 724-725, 728-729, 730; Cherin (1788), 338-341, 355-357, 361-363, 369-370, 376; Maugard (1788), 117; Grolée-Virville (1978), 23, 36, 54, 61, 63, 71, 72, 75, 76-78, 177-208, 210; Du Puy de Clinchamps (1978), 42-43. Examples of printed proofs of nobility made before the Juge d'Armes are in Gentil de Rosmorduc (1891); Ribier (1907-1912). See also Sereville and Saint Simon (1974), Plate IV.

(31)   Cherin (1788), 373-374, 402; Maugard (1788), 11-12, 18-19, 116;

Borel d'Hauterive (1849-1850), 272-314; (1864), 155, 157; (1866), 417-420; (1869), 378-380; La Roque and Barthélemy (1864), iii-vi; Durye (1974), 3; Grolée-Virville (1978), 84; Du Puy de Clinchamps (1978), 60-64. Examples of printed lists of persons whose nobility was proved before the Royal Genealogist are in La Roque and Barthélemy (1864); Borel d'Hauterive (1849-1850), 272-314. Lists of families whose nobility was registered in the West Indian Conseils Supérieurs have been printed in Thounens (1789), 82-86; Dessalles (1847-1848); La Roque and Barthélemy (1865), 14-23; Borel d'Hauterive (1866), 420-427; (1868), 381-405; (1869), 381-412; (1874), 261-267 (all these lists are incomplete).

Chapter 10 – Husband and Wife

(1) Mathieu (1946), 124; Fox-Davies (1949), 539, 577; D'Haucourt and Durivault (1965), 38; Innes and Innes (1978), 50, 84, 94.

(2) Heraldica (1940), 77; Innes and Innes (1978), 50, 83-84, 85. The influence of English thought has led to some modern writers supposing that the English rule forbidding married women using their arms except combined with their husbands' arms was of general application (e.g., Stevenson (1914) 333).

(3) Mathieu (1946), 126; D'Haucourt and Durivault (1965), 38.

(4) Dallaway (1793), 388; Seton (1863), 214; Fox-Davies (1949), 535; Brooke-Little (1978), 145,147; Innes and Innes (1978), 85. In 1950 an English herald stated that it was the general feeling that "marriage should not, and indeed cannot, deprive an armigerous lady of her right to her father's arms" but that it had never been decided how to put this into effect "without contravening any of the old rules"; the matter, he stated, was "at present under consideration" (The Coat of Arms I (1950), No.4, 115).

(5) Heraldica (1940), 75, 77; Innes (1940C), 362-363; Innes and Innes (1978), 50, 66, 69, 75, 81, 82.

(6) Marshall (1882), 34-35; Harwood (1916), 116-120; Fox-Davies (1949), 538; Brooke-Little (1978), 145; Squibb (1981), 477-478.

(7) Du Boscq de Beaumont (1906), 170; Mathieu (1946), 146-147, 150.

(8) Mathieu (1946), 124; Fox-Davies (1949), 539, 577; D'Haucourt and Durivault (1965), 38; Innes and Innes (1978), 50, 85; Brooke-Little (1978), 147.

(9)   Mathieu (1946), 124-127; Fox-Davies (1949), 535; D'Haucourt and Durivault (1965), 38; Innes and Innes (1978), 50, 83-85; Brooke-Little (1978), 145, 147. For samples of what was registered in the Armorial Général, see Prevost (1910), passim; (1913), passim; (1922-1924), passim; Meurgey de Tupigny (1965-1967), passim.

(10)   Segoing (1657), 33; Borel d'Hauterive (1843), 371; Mathieu (1946), 125; Fox-Davies (1949), 539,578; Innes and Innes (1978), 84, 85; Brooke-Little (1978), 139-148.

(11)   Edmondson (1780) I, 179-180; Dallaway (1793), 370; Woodward and Burnett (1892), 486, 523, 526; Fox-Davies (1949), 523, 526, 531-543; Squibb (1956), 103; (1959), 190; Brooke-Little (1978), 139.142, 147, 148, 204.

(12)   Mackenzie (1680), 80-81; Nisbet (1722-1742) II, 34-35, 37, 38; Edmondson (1780) I, 179; Woodward and Burnett (1892), 486, 523, 526; Fox-Davies (1949), 541; Innes and Innes (1978), 50, 51, 53, 78-79, 80, 84, 85. When inescutcheons were used in ancient Scottish heraldry, they served a different purpose, for example to contain the paternal arms over a shield composed of the arms of fiefs or of heiresses.

(13)   Boisseau (1657), 2; Mackenzie (1680), 81; Menestrier (1696), 214; Woodward and Burnett (1892), 504-505; Prinet (1909), 374-382; Mathieu (1946), 124-127; D'Haucourt and Durivault. (1965), 38; Galbreath and Jéquier (1977), 231, 232. There were many simultaneous registrations of the arms of husbands and wives in the Armorial Général of 1696-1709; they were usually in the form "X ... and Y ... his wife bear ... accollee with ..."; for samples see Meurgey de Tupigny (1965-1967), passim. For examples of the use of accollee shields by a wife, see Bosredon (1892), 34; Galbreath and Jéquier (1977), 143, 231; by a husband, see Bosredon (1892), 72. When inescutcheons were used in French heraldry, they often contained the paternal arms placed over a shield containing the quartered arms of alliances. For examples of impaled shields, see Magneney (1633), 147, 152, 195-208.

Chapter 11 – Timbres and Accessories

(1)   The word "timbre" originally meant a crest. It was still occasionally used in this sense in England and Scotland in the sixteenth century. In France crests were generally abandoned in the sixteenth century, and thereafter the word "timbre" was applied to a helm, or sometimes a coronet. When crests began to be used again from the seventeenth century, they were called "cimiers". The meaning of "timbre" appears to have changed also in Britain, where it was used

with the modern French meaning as recently as the nineteenth century. We use it here in this sense (primarily a helm with or without its mantling, or sometimes a coronet), so that by "timbred arms" we mean a shield of arms surmounted by a helm which may be provided with a mantling, or by a coronet. See Moreau (1630), 27-30; Segoing (1657), 468-470; Boisseau (1657), 26, 48; Geliot and Palliot (1661), 630; Menestrier (1661), 182; (1665), 42, 44; Guillim (1666), 394; Barbier (1856), 361; Seton (1863), 72-73, 77, 201, 216; Marshall (1882), 35; Innes (1940E), 198; Mathieu (1946), 206; Wagner (1956), 78, 126.

(2)   As early as the thirteenth century there were some non-nobles in certain parts of France (especially the north-east of the country) who used armorial seals. Some have seen this use, which seems to have grown with time, as an indication that it was lawful for non-nobles to use arms; others have seen it as an abuse. The nobles complained about it. The King himself went no further than to forbid the bearing of timbred arms by non-nobles.

(3)   Brisson and Charondas Le Caron (1609), 165vo.; Cadot (1697), 55-56; Brillon (1711) II, 792; La Roque (1734), Noblesse, 418, 419; D'Hozier, (1738-1768), Register I, Second Part, 665, 667, 675, 681; Bacquet (1744), 363; Cherin (1788) 46, 65, 69, 97, 122, 130-131, 134-136, 143-144, 239; Mathieu (1946), 48, 206-207; Adam (1957), 10; Galbreath and Jéquier (1977), 174, 194.

(4)   D'Hozier (1738-1768), Register I, Second Part, 678, 693, 702; Cherin (1788), 111-112, 133-134; Grandmaison (1904-1905) I, 9-10; Savage (1925), 380. An Edict of 1706 ennobling the Mayor of Paris gave him the title of chevalier and the right to bear timbred arms (Bluche and Durye (1962) I, 33).

(5)   Brisson and Charondas Le Caron (1609), 165vo.; Bouvot (1628) II, 46-47; Geliot and Palliot (1661), 369-371; Maugard (1788), 57; Mathieu (1946), 206, 207.

(6)   Mathieu (1946), 60, 207.

(7)   La Roque (1734), Noblesse, 90-91; Blanc (1975), 541-550. Almost all royal grants of timbred arms were made to persons who were already noble, or were made concurrently with grants of nobility; the rare exceptions may have all involved grantees who were thought in error to be already noble (cf. Blanc (1975), 546).

(8)   Ferrières and Boucher d'Argis (1787) I, 123-124; Cherin (1788), 20-21; Borel d'Hauterive (1859), 371-374; Du Boscq de Beaumont (1906), 167, 169-172; Mathieu (1946), 204-206; Bluche and Durye

(1962) I, 33; Meurgey de Tupigny (1965-1967) I, xxii. By a further misunderstanding, it was thought by some that the Letters Patent of 1371 had generally ennobled all the burgesses of Paris, and that Letters Patent of 1577 which accorded nobility to the Mayor ("Prévôt des Marchands") and Aldermen ("Echevins") of Paris had had a restrictive effect, whereas in fact the Letters Patent of 1577 would (if they had been registered and had thus become effective) have conferred on these offices an ennobling power which they had not hitherto possessed; it was not until 1706 that these offices effectively acquired this power (Bluche and Durye (1962) I, 33).

(9)   Grandmaison (1904-1905) II, 25-31, 40-49; Du Boscq de Beaumont (1906), 167-168, 170-173.

(10)   Ferrières and Boucher d'Argis (1787) II, 282; Tesson (1897), 17; Mathieu (1946), 88-89; Meurgey de Tupigny (1965-1967) I, xxii.

(11)   It seems that until 1672 ordinary Scottish gentlemen were not allowed helms (Innes and Innes (1978), 35). Even clergymen are entitled in law to a helm in England and in Scotland, although they often prefer to use a less war-like timbre.

(12)   In England, where in modern times almost all armigers use a crest, it is unusual to see a shield timbred with a helm unless a crest is also present. In Scotland it is still possible for a grant of arms not to include a crest, and shields timbred with a helm alone are seen. In France, where most armigers did not use a crest, it was common for shields to be timbred with a helm alone, or a helm with its mantling; such a practice was encouraged by the fact that the use of a helm was supposed to be a distinctive sign of nobility.

(13)   Guillim (1666), 395-396; Mackenzie (1680), 86; Nisbet (1722-1742) II, Part IV, 5; Edmondson (1780) I, 183; Seton (1863), 235-236; Woodward and Burnett (1892), 602; Fox-Davies (1949), 303, 319-322; Brooke-Little (1978), 154; Innes and Innes (1978), 17; Forrester (1983), 161.

(14)   Scohier (1597), 60; Moreau (1630), 28; Magneney (1633), passim; Geliot (1635), 218-220; Segoing (1657), 468-470; Boisseau (1657), 24, 26; Menestrier (1665), 42-43; (1696), 208; Mackenzie (1680), 86-87; Nisbet (1722-1742) II, Part IV, 5; Dupuy Demportes (1754) I, 101-102; Menestrier and Lemoine (1780), 234-235; Leber (1838), 290; Borel d'Hauterive (1843), 353-354; Martres (1847), Plate XII; D'Haucourt and Durivault (1965), 118-120.

(15)   Grandmaison (1904-1905), passim; Du Boscq de Beaumont (1906), 169-172. It was understood that descendants of an ennobled man

whose settlement of arms included a helm in profile could modify the helm as the generations passed, so that his son could set it at an angle, and his great-grandson could turn it further. If the settlement of arms concerned a person who had only personal and not hereditary nobility, it might have been expected that his non-noble descendants would have to give up the helm; however, it seems that the Juge d'Armes held the view that they could keep the helm, provided no change was made in its aspect, that is, provided it remained in profile.

(16)   Geliot and Palliot (1661), 370, 373.

(17)   Menestrier (1665), 43; Mackenzie (1680), 89; Nisbet (1722-1742) II, Part IV, 8-9; Dupuy Demportes (1754) I, 119; Edmondson (1780) I, 184; Borel d'Hauterive (1843), 354, 359; Du Boscq de Beaumont (1906), 169-170; Fox-Davies (1949), 391-393; D'Haucourt and Durivault (1965), 120-123; Innes and Innes (1978), 18.

(18)   Galbreath and Jéquier (1977), 184-188.

(19)   Guillim (1666), 422, 423, 430-449; Mackenzie (1680), 92; Nisbet (1722-1742) II, Part IV, 49-50; Seton (1863), 232; Fox-Davies (1949), 363; Squibb (1959), 72.

(20)   Maugard (1788), 57; Cherin (1788), 138, 247; Borel d'Hauterive (1845), 269-271; (1857), 341; Mathieu (1946), 209-210; Adam (1957), 10; Galbreath and Jéquier (1977), 194.

(21)   Scohier (1597), 65-66; Favyn (1620) I, 74; Moreau (1630), 39-40; Magneney (1633), passim; Geliot (1635), 83, 129-130; 209-210; Varennes (1640), 576-578; Boisseau (1657), 24-25; Segoing (1660), passim; Geliot and Palliot (1661), 206-209, 372-373; Menestrier (1665), 43-44; (1696), 207-208; Mackenzie (1680), 92; Nisbet (1722-1742) II, Part IV, 46-48; Dupuy Demportes (1754) I, 117-118; Menestrier and Lemoine (1780), 232; Edmondson (1780) I, 198; Borel d'Hauterive (1843), 357-358; Martres (1847), Plate XII; Woodward and Burnett (1892), 623-625; Fox-Davies (1949) 365-368; D'Haucourt and Durivault (1965), 122-125; Galbreath and Jéquier (1977), 186-188; Brooke-Little (1978), 186-187; Innes and Innes (1978), 26.

(22)   Fox-Davies (1949), 373-376; Innes and Innes (1978), 19; Moncreiffe (1982), 16. The "crest coronets" with which we are concerned are the conventional ones with four fleurons or "strawberry leaves", three of which are visible in representations, and not the various other "crest coronets" sometimes used for special reasons in modern British heraldry (cf. Fox-Davies (1949), 376-378; Innes and Innes (1978), 19).

(23)   Edmondson (1780) I, 198; Innes (1946), 152-156; Fox-Davies (1949), 378-381; Innes and Innes (1978), 18; Forrester (1983), 158-159.

(24)   Magneney (1633), 106-108, 155-162; Boisseau (1657), 27; Dupuy Demportes (1754) I, 131; Galbreath and Jéquier (1977), 122, 189, 231.

(25)   Segoing (1657), 466; Geliot and Palliot (1661), 207, 371; Borel d'Hauterive (1843), 355; (1845), 269-270; (1857), 340-341, 344-349; Barbier (1856), 361; Prevost (1910), vii; Olivier and Vialet (1927), passim; Mathieu (1946), 209; Galbreath and Jéquier (1977), 188-189; Dupuy de Clinchamps (1978), 104.

(26)   Du Boscq de Beaumont (1906), 169-170, 172.

(27)   Fox-Davies (1949), 336-338. See also various grants in Howard (1866-1902); Bannerman (1904-1916); Clarke (1916-1938); Littledale (1925-1926); etc.

(28)   Innes and Innes (1978), 19, 35.

(29)   Du Boscq de Beaumont (1906), 172-173; Mathieu (1946), 202; D'Haucourt and Durivault (1965), 24-26; Galbreath and Jéquier (1977), 179-180. The abandoning of crests in the seventeenth century is evidenced by the achievements of arms blazoned in several handsome books of the period. One such book (Le Feron and Godefroy (1658)) contains elaborate achievements of the arms of all the Constables, Chancellors, Marshals and Admirals of France from early times until the seventeenth century. The shield of each Constable is timbred with a ducal crown above which is a barred helm facing the front (with a mantling); instead of a crest there is another, smaller ducal crown on the helm. All the other shields are surmounted by a helm (and mantling) resembling that of the Constables. Each Chancellor has a "mortier" resting on his helm. The Marshals and the Admirals have arrangements of plumes on their helms; these resemble crests, but there is nothing individual about them - in fact, the same arrangement is used for all. On the other hand a somewhat earlier book (Magneney (1633)) contains a proportion of crested achievements. Of about fifty eighteenth century settlements of arms for ennobled persons in Grandmaison (1904-1905), only one (I, 95) seems to include a crest.

(30)   Moreau (1630), 41, Varennes (1640), 579; Boisseau (1657), 26; Menestrier (1696), 265; Dallaway (1793), 388; Seton (1863), 214; Howard (1888), Frontispiece; Innes (1938 B), 121; Heraldica (1940), 94-95; Mathieu (1946), 43, 209; Fox-Davies (1949), 62, 535, 572; Brooke-Little (1978), 13, 148, 162.

(31) Seton (1863), 130, 214-215; Stevenson (1914), 181-182; Innes (1929), 556; (1938 B), 121; Heraldica (1.940), 94-95; Innes and Innes (1978), 19, 50-51, 58, 83 (and see the Second Edition (1956), Plates XXXII-XXXIII).

(32) Innes and Innes (1978), 51.

(33) Moreau (1630), 41; Varennes (1640), 579; Menestrier (1696), 265; Mathieu (1946), 43, 209; Fox-Davies (1949), 366-367, 532; Galbreath and Jéquier (1977), 230; Innes and Innes (1978), 83.

(34) Favyn (1620) I, 61; Magneney (1633), 195-208; Varennes (1640), 599-600; Boisseau (1657), 26,42; Geliot and Palliot (1661), 191, 193, 371; Menestrier (1696), 214, 266; Dupuy Demportes (1754) I, 77; Cherin (1788), 239-240; Stevenson (1914), 255-256; Mathieu (1946), 211; Fox-Davies (1949), 579; D'Haucourt and Durivault (1965), 126; Galbreath and Jéquier (1977), 231; Innes and Innes (1978), 84 (and see the Second Edition (1956), Plate XXXII).

(35) Borel d'Hauterive (1843), 365-368; Du Boscq de Beaumont (1906), 173; Mathieu (1946), 211; Galbreath and Jéquier (1977), 214.

(36) Edmondson (1780) I, 190; Fox-Davies (1949), 448, 572; Brooke-Little (1978), 175.

(37) Seton (1863), 240; Fox-Davies (1949), 448; Innes and Innes (1978), 20, 83; Brooke-Little (1978), 175.

(38) Guillim (1666), 407; Mackenzie (1680), 94; Edmondson (1780) I, 198; Seton (1863), 273-275; Howard (1877), 184; (1884), 189; (1888), Plate following 168; (1890), 88; (1892), 89; Woodward and Burnett (1892), 646-647, 750-751; Paul (1903), xix; Stevenson (1914), 85-86, 227-251, 311-332, 344-350, Plate VI; Littledale (1925), 33-34, 82-84, 93-94, 103-104; (1926), 135-136, 200-203; Fox-Davies (1949), 419-428, 572; Squibb (1956), 60; (1959), 138; Galbreath and Jéquier (1977), 197-198; Brooke-Little (1978), 179; Innes and Innes (1978), 50, 51, 71-74; Dennys (1982), 55, 177.

(39) Segoing (1657), 472; Borel d'Hauterive (1843), 363; Du Boscq de Beaumont (1906), 172-173; Mathieu (1946), 210.

(40) Bara (1628), 6; Boisseau (1657), 2; Menestrier (1696), 19-20; Cadot (1697), Plate I; Armorial Général (1696-1709), Volumes of Painted Arms; Nisbet (1722-1742) I, 11; Borel d'Hauterive (1843), 369-370; Grazebrook (1890), 69-70, 74, Plate I; Woodward and Burnett (1892), 56; Galbreath and Jéquier (1977), 81, 85.

(41)   Boisseau (1657), 2; Menestrier (1696), 20, 214, 266; Armorial Général (1696-1709), Volumes of Painted Arms; Cadot (1697), Plate II; Nisbet (1722-1742) I, 12; II, 35; Dupuy Demportes (1754) I, 77; Edmondson (1780) I, 178; Borel d'Hauterive (1843), 370; Seton (1863), 208-211, 214; Woodward and Burnett (1892), 58, 476-477; Stevenson (1914), 136; Innes (1941), 133; Mathieu (1946), 199-200; Fox-Davies (1949), 533-535, 572-573; Hope and Wagner (1953), 32; Galbreath and Jéquier (1977), 84, 89-90, 231; Innes and Innes (1978), 83-84; Brooke-Little (1978), 20, 147.

Chapter 12 - "Tokens of Nobleness"

(1)   Sitwell (1902), 62-77, 89-291; Wagner (1956), 77; McFarlane (1973), 6-9, 122-125, 142-143, 268-269, 275.

(2)   It was mainly antiquaries and lawyers like Camden and Coke who still referred in the seventeenth century to gentlemen and all whose ancestors bore arms as forming part of the body of nobles. A judgement of the Court of Chivalry in a case of 1639 recited that the Kings of Arms and heralds had the right to direct the funerals of gentlemen and noblemen below the rank of baron (Squibb (1956), 41). Contemporary English heralds, desirous of avoiding possible misunderstanding, and anxious not to revive the battles over "nobiles minores" which afflicted English heraldry sixty or eighty years ago, generally eschew the word "noble". In a recent book edited by one English herald, it is stated that "an "armiger" ranks as a gentleman, a degree which can be regarded in all but name as a form of lesser nobility", while another says, under the heading "noble", that "in heraldry any armigerous person, of whatever rank, is *nobilis* (i.e., "known"), though in common usage the word "noble" applies only to the peerage" (D.H.B.Chesshyre in C.A. von Volborth, Heraldry of the World (1973), 181, 191; Brooke-Little (1978), 339).

(3)   Du Puy de Clinchamps (1978) contains a useful and generally accurate summary of French nobiliary law and custom. The brief notes in Ferrières and Boucher d'Argis (1787) II, 278-285, 333, and in Marion (1923), 392-399, provide a generalised overview of the subject, without accuracy of detail. On ennoblement by the tenure of civil and military posts, the authority is Bluche and Durye (1962). A concise discussion of some aspects of the nobility of Brittany is Meyer (1972). For social life and differences, especially in the eighteenth century, Chaussinand-Nogaret (1976) is of interest.

(4)   French nobles were expected to assert their nobility by using these basic titles in formal documents. Omitting them systematically over a long period of time might be taken as a renunciation of the noble

state. This applied in France, where any noble was entitled to use these titles without having to prove his right thereto unless he was challenged (for example during a nobiliary survey). It did not apply in territories such as the French West Indies, where it had been decreed that no one was to use any noble title, on pain of being fined, unless his nobility had previously been registered at the local Conseil Supérieur (sovereign court). In these islands the nobles had no privileges of substance (except a partial exemption from a particular tax which most nobles enjoyed anyway by virtue of their positions in the militia or in the judiciary) and the long process of proof before the Royal Genealogist: and registration by the Conseil Supérieur was very onerous. In 1789 the Royal Genealogist approved the nobility of a family which had resided in Guadeloupe since the seventeenth century and which now sought to register its nobility. The fact that the family had abstained from using any noble title for over a century was successfully explained away on the ground that any use of such titles prior to registration would have been illegal (Borel d'Hauterive (1864), 155-157; (1866), 417-420; (1867), 169-172).

(5)   It was common, especially among the richer or more pretentious of the nobles in the eighteenth century, for titles of baron, viscount, count or marquis to be assumed; such assumed titles had no legal validity but as they in fact brought no additional privileges those who used them were generally unmolested (Du Puy de Clinchamps (1978), 58-60), This practice, which became still more common in the nineteenth century, is the origin of most titles borne nowadays in France by those of noble descent. Perhaps still more common nowadays are such titles which are used by persons who are not of noble descent (Du Puy de Clinchamps (1978), 96, 111).

(6)   Squibb (1956), 21-22, 84; (1959), 176-177.

(7)   Mackenzie (1680), 14.

(8)   For various aspects of "Dérogeance" see for example Brillon (1711) II, 788; La Roque (1734), Noblesse, 115, 355-369, 383, 409, 411, 413; Ferrières and Boucher d'Argis (1787) II, 282-283; Cherin (1788), xxxv-xxxviii, 45, 91, 95, 113-114, 115, 119, 120-121, 151, 162, 165, 181, 191, 227-230, 336; La Bigne de Villeneuve (1918), 78-81, 101-102; Bluche and Durye (1962) I, 42-45; Du Puy de Clinchamps (1978), 45-46; Arundel de Condé (1981), 143, 147-151. See also Notes 9 and 10.

(9)   La Roque (1734), Noblesse, 111, 368-369; Ferrières and Boucher d'Argis (1787) II, 283; Cherin (1788), xxxv-xxxvi; La Bigne de Villeneuve (1918), 134-135; Du Puy de Clinchamps (1978), 46-47; Meyer (1972), 56, 78-92.

(10) La Roque (1734), Noblesse, 136, 256, 409-410; Ferrières and Boucher d'Argis (1787) II, 283; Cherin (1788), 45, 177, 186, 254-255, 292-293, 328, 349; La Bigne de Villeneuve (1918) 81-83, 90-100, 105-108; Cameron and Polaczek (1938), 63-64; Meyer (1972), 82-88.

(11) We are concerned only with families whose nobility in a first country was accepted as proof of its nobility in a second country. There are of course many other families which were noble in one country and were subsequently noble in another country, but in at least some cases the nobility in the second country may have been based on their services or other distinctions in the second country rather than on any nobility they may have brought with them.

(12) For some examples of such families see C.Baschi, Marquis d'Aubais, and L.Menard, Pieces Fugitives pour servir a L'Histoire de France (1759) I, Part 2, Jugemens sur la Noblesse, 2; Jougla (1934-1952) IV, 284, 487; VI, 172, 245, 509; Lart (1938), 16-18, 76-89, 150-155, 162, 169-182; Meyer (1966), 1018-1029, 1040, 1048-1049; Le Second Ordre (1973), 179-184; Arundel de Condé (1981), 144, 169. Proof that the family had been noble in its country of origin might involve a genealogical certificate from a King of Arms, or sworn testimony from reputable members of the British nobility and gentry that the family in question was one of theirs, or a certificate of nobility issued by a British Sovereign (the exiled Stewarts helped several of their followers in this way); see for example Cherin (1788), 429-431; Ruvigny (1904), 191, 195-213, 221; and some of the above references in Baschi and Menard; Lart; Le Second Ordre; and Arundel de Condé.

(13) Jougla (1934-1952) I, 199 (No.962-964); IV, 494 (No.22279); Lart (1938), 76-88; Le Second Ordre (1973), 183, 184; Sereville and Saint Simon (1975), 113. Although there seems to be no record of any family recently emigrated from England being admitted to Court Honours (no doubt because few ancient English families followed the Stewarts), several Irish families were admitted.

(14) Cherin (1788), 177; Arundel de Condé (1981), 168, 169.

(15) Howard and Chester (1880), 100, 146, 148; (1883), 1, 99-100, 119, 308.

(16) Examples of such families appear to include Villettes (see Jougla (1934-1952) VI, 476; Rabino (1940)); Spon (see Burke's Landed Gentry, Eighteenth Edition, Volume II (1969), 155-157; Sereville and Saint Simon (1977), 351). It seems that proof of possession of foreign arms may not be sufficient, and that proof of foreign nobility is also

required (this presumably applies in the case of a country where it is possible to have arms without being noble - as in France); see Cassubian (1966).

(17)   Innes and Innes (1978), 48-49 (see also the Second Edition (1956), 92, Note 2). When matriculating arms of English or French origin, the Lord Lyon may difference them as he would do for arms of Scottish origin in conformity with Scottish law which requires the proper distinctions to be made between the head of a family and the various cadets (see Chapter 8).

(18)   Squibb (1956), 9, 20; (1959), 170.

(19)   Markland (1865), 152; Sitwell (1902), 80; Squibb (1956), passim; (1959), 139-140, 170-177, 193, 199; Brooke-Little (1969), Note 2. According to Guillim (1666), 409, the "gentlemen without arms" included "some by blood, some by office, some by sacred academical dignity".

(20)   Squibb (1956), 6, 28-32; (1959), 170-177; Brooke-Little (1969), Note 2. J.H.Round, who is sometimes cited as an opponent of the principle that there is a connection between arms and gentility, was certainly opposed to the idea that a grant of arms could in itself convert a non-gentleman into a gentleman, but he appears to have accepted that it was the possession of gentility which led to the receipt of a grant of arms (Round (1910) II, 321-322).

(21)   Howard (1876), 312-313; (1880), 298; (1886), 99; Bannerman (1910), 273; (1914), 120-121, 265, 266, 267; Littledale (1925), 2-3; Clarke (1929-1931), 153; Wagner (1956), 60-61, 72-82, 125, 137-138, and passim; Brooke-Little (1969), Note 2. That only "noblemen" could assume arms in "the earliest period" was a view also held by Sir T. Innes of Learney (The Armorial House or Family, in Notes and Queries CLXXVII (1939) (September), 164).

(22)   Howard (1888), Plate after page 200; (1894), 329; Schomberg (1908), 138-139; Rylands (1911), 159-160; Bannerman (1914), 268, 269; (1916), 286-287; Littledale (1925), 3,6,41-44,53-54, 92-93, 96-97, 114-115; (1926), 149-150, 176; Wagner (1956), 77-81, 125-126.

(23)   Wagner (1956), 76, 77, 79-81, 90, 96-99.

(24)   Wagner (1956), 9-10; Squibb (1985), 130-131.

(25)   Wagner (1956), 98-99. That the Crown believed arms and nobility to be connected is confirmed by a reference to royal Letters Patent of

Edward VI in which arms are described as "signs and tokens of nobility" (Littledale (1926), 163-164.).

(26)   Howard (1868), 46-47, 231, 281-282; (1874) 408; (1876), 261-262, 311-313; (1877), 55; (1886), 269-270; (1888), Plate after page 272; (1892), 161-162; (1896), 97; (1898), 156, 193-194; (1900), 141; Harwood (1905), 187-188; (1911), 222-223; Bannerman (1906), 1-2; (1908), 145; (1914), 1-2; (1916), 245-246, 287-288; (1916-7), 26, 60; Littledale (1925), 5, 11-12, 26-27, 35-37, 50-51, 62-63, 69, 75-76, 77-79, 81-82, 112-114; (1926), 125, 128-129, 136-137, 152-153, 162, 167-168, 1,78, 195-196; Clarke (1929-1931), 357; (1935-1937), 171-172.

(27)   Howard (1868), 228-229; (1877), 121, 311; (1884) 109-110; (1896), 60; Littledale (1925), 14-15, 25-26; (1926), 141-142, 144, 205-207; Clarke (1935-1937), 288.

(28)   Howard (1876), 43, 251; (1880), 447; (1884), 1-2, 92-93; (1886), 53-54, 133; (1888), 324-325; (1892), 91; Bannerman (1906), Plate after page 212; (1908), 196; (1910), 230-231; Clarke (1916-1917), 259; (1918-1919, 1-2; (1929-1931), 238; Littledale (1925), 76-77; (1926), 206-207.

(29)   Howard (1888), 59; Wagner (1956), 79; Squibb (1981), 448.

(30)   Howard (1874), 349-350, 371-372, 397; (1876), 191-192; (1890), 72-73; (1892), 136; (1894), 49; (1898), 101-102; Baildon (1904) (July), 55; Littledale (1925), 99-100; Squibb (1956), 58, 59; Wagner (1956), 9-10, 59,78-79, 88,89,137, 162; (1967), 294-295.

(31)   Nicholls (1863), 466; Squibb (1956), 59; Wagner (1956), 98-99; Dennys (1982), 155.

(32)   Squibb (1956), 33, 59. In 1605 commissioners appointed to perform the office of Earl Marshal were given power to revoke grants of arms made unlawfully or unworthily by the heralds (Round (1910) I, 100-101).

(33)   Seton (1863), 355; P (1955) 147; Full Report (1955), 41-42, 54, 56-57.

(34)   Sitwell (1902), 83, 91; Heraldica (1940), 132; Innes (1941A), 129.

(35)   Act (1592); Seton (1863), 54.

(36)   Mackenzie (1680), 11-12. Mackenzie is regarded as a particularly authoritative commentator on the heraldic law of Scotland (cf. the comment of a judge of the Court of Session cited in Innes (1941B), 2).

(37)   Act (1672).

(38)   Act (1672); Seton (1863), 57, 285, 490-492; Stevenson (1914), 81, 451-455.

(39)   Mackenzie (1680), 12-15 (discussed in, for example, Seton (1863), 57-58; Stevenson (1914), 34-35, 82; Innes (1940A), 254). In a note to his countrymen prefaced to his book, Mackenzie says that he had been intimate with a learned advocate at Bourges in France, who was admired all over Europe for his skill in heraldry. It may be of interest to compare Mackenzie's categories of persons having "virtue" with the French rules about the nobility of such persons.

With regard to those who held land of the Crown, many French nobles held royal fiefs and this was considered so usual an accompaniment of noble status that, until the King stopped this in 1579, any non-nobles who held fiefs were automatically ennobled provided they satisfied certain conditions.

With regard to soldiers having "considerable command" an Edict of 1600 had clarified the French law by providing that two successive generations of the rank of captain would automatically confer nobility on non-noble soldiers. This rule was still being applied during the nobiliary survey of 1666 but it then appears to have fallen into disuse, until it was revived in a more restrictive form by an Edict of 1750 (which prescribed that full nobility would be acquired if three successive generations of a family held at least the rank of captain, provided that each generation had either died before leaving the service, or had become a Chevalier of the Order of St. Louis and had served at least 30 years or had had to retire because of wounds) (La Roque (1734), Noblesse, 170, 403-404; Cherin (1788), 8284, 364-372; Bluche and Durye (1962) II, 35-43; Blanc (1975), 541; Arundel de Condé (1981), 15-17).

With regard to clergymen, French priests belonged to the First Order of the nation (the nobles formed the Second Order) and were not normally considered to be part of the nobility. As they were celibate, the question of hereditary nobility did not arise.

With regard to doctors of universities, the doctors of French universities sometimes claimed that they were automatically ennobled by their doctorates, but although it tolerated the use in some places (for example in Lyons) of the epithet "Noble" placed before the name, the Crown refused to accept that French doctorates conferred nobility on those who were not born noble. Perhaps somewhat unfairly, the French Crown accepted that two successive generations of doctorates of law of the University of Avignon were sufficient to ennoble a family; Avignon was under the sovereignty of the Pope and the French Crown accepted that the local customary law was effective (Bluche and Durye (1962) II, 47; Du Puy de Clinchamps (1978), 30-31).

With regard to advocates (anglice: barristers) their profession was considered to be very compatible with nobility, but it did not actually ennoble those advocates who were not already noble. The same may be said of physicians. Those advocates who became "Conseillers" (judges) of a sovereign court were automatically entitled to the privileges of nobility; depending on the court, ennoblement became complete after one or two generations (Cherin (1788), 176, 262; Bluche and Durye (1962) II, 15-25).

As for orators and poets, their occupations were not in themselves ennobling, but many poets were noble by birth, while others were given Letters Patent of ennoblement by the King, or were provided with ennobling posts.

In England, all the occupations mentioned by Mackenzie would seem to qualify a man for a grant of arms. In particular, an English confirmation of arms made in 1616 by Clarenceux Camden stated that the beneficiary was "ennobled by the dignity of the doctorate of sacred theology", and later Guillim included the gentlemen" by sacred academical dignity" among those persons who were indeed gentlemen although they might not yet be in possession of arms (Guillim (1666), 409; Littledale (1926), 205-206).

It is interesting to see how the possession of wealth was treated in the three countries. Mackenzie says that "riches do not nobilitate" and do not in themselves justify a grant of arms from Lyon, although he concedes that "nobility is nothing ofttimes but ancient riches" (which seems to be an acknowledgement that the inheritance of wealth may give the opportunity to integrate oneself into the nobility) (Mackenzie (1680), 13). In France wealth did not in itself bring nobility, but those who had it were often able to purchase one of the posts which brought automatic nobility. A favourite post was that of "Conseiller Secrétaire du Roi" (or just "Secrétaire du Roi") which is not to be confused with the high office of secretary of state and which required practically no qualifications and involved practically no duties, so that in the course of time most such posts came to be acquired by rich non-nobles in pursuit of nobility (Bluche and Durye (1962) II, 1-14; Meyer (1972), 119-131; Du Puy de Clinchamps (1978), 25--27. In England, it seems to have been accepted from a relatively early date that possessions and riches were sufficient to justify a grant of arms, provided the person concerned was not of "vile blood" or a rebel or heretic, as may be seen from the royal Letters Patent of 1530 in favour of Clarenceux.

As for merchants and those who exercise "mean trades", they have been discussed already.

(40)   Howard (1874), 356; (1877), 395; (1884), 179, 189; (1886), 259; X (1900), 165-171; Bannerman (1910), 1; (1916), 1; Clarke (1916-1917), 253-256 (1926-1928), 9; Littledale (1925), 79-80, 82-83, 124; Lart (1938), 78-84, 150-155; Cameron and Polaczek (1938), 52, 59-60; Innes (1940E), 185, 194; (1946), 126-128; Grant (1945), Introduction; Innes and Innes (1978), 97-100, Plate III.

(41)   Innes (1940A), 273-274, 296; (1940D), 363; (1940E), 194; Gayre (1958), 82; Innes and Innes (1978), 13, 49; "Saltire Argent" (1979), 10. The form of words in the passage quoted from modern Scottish grants of arms is somewhat reminiscent of the forms of words found in some English grants of the sixteenth century (Howard (1868), 231, 281-282; (1886), 269-270; (1888), Plate after page 200; Clarke (1935-1937), 171-172).

(42)   La Roque (1734), Noblesse, 90-91; Blanc (1975), 546.

(43)   Brillon (1711) II, 786; La Bigne de Villeneuve (1918), 115; Mathieu (1946), 50, 53, 59, 231-239; Du Puy de Clinchamps (1978), 45.

(44)   With regard to Scotland, see for example Mackenzie (1680), 14, 78; Stevenson (1914), 68, 451; Innes (1940E), 193. In England, a plaintiff in the Court of Chivalry in the first half of the seventeenth century asserted that the defendant could not be a gentleman because the Court of Star Chamber had sentenced his father to the pillory, which made the father and his posterity incapable of assuming the dignity of gentleman or of bearing arms. Unfortunately nothing further is recorded about this case (Squibb (1956), 23).

(45)   Borel d'Hauterive (1845), 271; Du Boscq de Beaumont (1906), 176; Mathieu (1946), 243-246; Galbreath and Jéquier (1977), 56; Grolée-Virville (1978), 95-96.

(46)   Borel d'Hauterive (1868), 360-362; (1877), 325-327; (1883), 341-343; Mathieu (1946), 247-257; D'Haucourt and Durivault (1965), 41-42.

(47)   Although the French laws of arms which have been discussed herein no longer form part of the law of France (or of any territory over which French sovereignty was maintained in the nineteenth and twentieth centuries), they survive as part of the corpus of law of some of the territories which passed from French sovereignty at an earlier

time and which have not altered (or have restored) that part of their law. An example of such a territory with which the present writer happens to be familiar is the island of St. Lucia in the West Indies. During most of the second half of the eighteenth century, St. Lucia was one of the French Windward Island colonies, with its own Court of Seneschalcy, subject to appeals to the Conseil Supérieur of Martinique (which was one of the "sovereign" courts mentioned in Chapter 3). The general laws of the French monarchy relating to nobility and arms formed part of the law of these colonies, to which were added a few particular enactments on nobility in these colonies, such as that mentioned in Note 4. Colonists who were ennobled by Letters Patent were provided by the Juge d'Armes with the usual settlements of arms. In the course of the wars which followed the French Revolution, St. Lucia was captured by the British Crown, which restored most of the pre-revolutionary law. In particular, a Proclamation of 1 July 1800 restored "the laws and customs and the regulations (Règlements) of the French Monarchy" (subject to some exceptions which are irrelevant here). This Proclamation also restored the Seneschalcy "as it was under the French Monarchy", and created a Court of Appeal or Conseil Supérieur to hear appeals "in conformity with the laws, customs and regulations of the French Monarchy followed and observed in the Windward Islands and the rights, honours and privileges attached thereto in accordance with the Ordinances of His French Majesty". In 1802 the Treaty of Amiens gave St. Lucia to the French Republic. However, the island was again captured by British forces in 1803, and another Proclamation, of 28 July 1803, restored the Conseil Supérieur and ordered that the provisions of the Proclamation of 1800 were to remain in force for the time being. An opinion of Counsel (Sir S. Romilly, K.C., Solicitor-General of England, and A.Pigott) produced for the British Government on 30 April 1806 stated that the Constitution of St. Lucia established by the Proclamation of 1803 was valid and in force. The British King had accepted, as his own laws, those of the French King before 1789 (although he could change them at any time if he so decided). The possession of St. Lucia by the British Crown was confirmed by the Treaty of Paris in May 1816. In 1826 a Commission of Inquiry into the Administration of Civil and Criminal Justice in the British West Indies found that St. Lucia still retained its old French law. Cases on appeal from St. Lucian courts to the Privy Council (for example, Du Boulay v. Du Boulay (1869) 6 Moore P.C. (N.S.), 31) have proceeded on the basis that St. Lucia continues to be subject to the old French colonial law, except where this has been changed by legislation. Not only have the laws of arms of the French Monarchy remained unchanged to this day in St. Lucia, but also they have remained within the jurisdiction of the courts. It will be recalled that in the French system the normal royal courts had jurisdiction in matters of nobility and arms. The St. Lucian courts established by the

Proclamations of 1800 and 1803 were invested with all the powers of the French royal courts. Since 1816 there have been several changes in the machinery for the administration of justice, but each newly constituted system of courts appears to have inherited the judicial powers of its predecessors.

GENERAL BIBLIOGRAPHY

This is not a complete bibliography of all relevant material, but a table of most of the sources mentioned in the Notes. It has seemed convenient to give separate lists of items in English and in French.

ENGLISH LANGUAGE

Act (1592)

Concerning the Office of Lyon King of Arms and his brother Heralds. This Act of the Parliament of Scotland (1592, c.125 or cap.29) is nowadays cited as the Lyon King of Arms Act 1592. It is printed for example in Mackenzie (1680), 11; Seton (1863), 493-495; Stevenson (1914), 436-437; The Acts of the Parliaments of Scotland 1424-1707, Second Revised Edition (1966), 51-52; Innes and Innes (1978), 122.

Act (1669)

Ratification in favour of the Lord Lyon King of Arms etc. This Act of the Parliament of Scotland (1669, c.95) is nowadays cited as the Lyon King of Arms Act 1669. It is printed for example in The Acts of the Parliaments of Scotland 1424-1707, Second Revised Edition (1966), 91-92.

Act (1672)

Act concerning the Privileges of the Office of Lyon King at Arms. This Act of the Parliament of Scotland (1672, c.21 or cap.47) is nowadays cited as the Lyon King of Arms Act 1672. It is printed for example in Seton (1863), 498-500; Stevenson (1914), 439-441; The Acts of the Parliaments of Scotland, Second Revised Edition (1966), 100-101; Innes and Innes (1978), 123-124.

Act (1867)

An Act to regulate the Court and Office of the Lyon King of Arms in Scotland. This Act of the British Parliament (30 and 31 Vict.c.17) is nowadays cited as the Lyon King of Arms Act 1867. It is printed for example in The Statutes of the United Kingdom 30 & 31 Victoria, 1867 (The Statutes at Large CVIII) (1867), 78-82; Stevenson (1914), 441-443; The Statutes, Revised Edition VIII (1950).

Armytage (1910)

Armytage (Sir G.J.), A Visitation of the County of Surrey, begun ... MDCLXII finished MDCLXVIII (Harleian Society Publications LX) (1910).

171

Baildon (1904)

Baildon (N.P.), Heralds' College and Prescription, in The Ancestor VIII (January 1904), 113-144; IX (April 1904), 214-224; X (July 1904), 52-69.

Bannerman (1904-1916)

Bannerman (W.B.), Editor, Miscellanea Genealogica et Heraldica. The years cited are those on the title pages of the bound volumes edited by him or (1916 only) by him and Clarke. Earlier volumes were edited by Howard (q.v.), later ones by Clarke (q.v.)

Barron (1902-1905)

Barron (A.O.), Editor, The Ancestor I-XII (1902-1905). Some specific items by other persons are cited under their names.

Brooke-Little (1969)

Brooke-Little (J.P.B.), Notes in A Complete Guide to Heraldry, by A.C.Fox-Davies, Annotated Edition (1969).

Brooke-Little (1978)

Brooke-Little (J.P.B.), Boutell's Heraldry, Revised Edition (1978).

Bruce (1980)

Bruce (E.), The Coronation of Sir Alexander Erskine of Cambo as Lord Lyon, in The Double Tressure (1980), 14-16.

Butcher (1926)

Butcher (B.), et al., Hastings or Hastinges, in The Complete Peerage, New Edition VI (1926), 345-369.

Cameron and Polaczek (1938)

Cameron (A.I.) and Polaczek (H.), Diploma of Nobility of Thomas Cumming, 1727, in The Juridical Review (1938), 51-74.

Cassubian (1966)

A Cassubian Coat of Arms, in The Coat of Arms IX (No.65) (1966), 2-4.

CHA (1879)

C.H.A., Disclaimers at the Visitation of Kent, 1665, in The Genealogist III (1879), 206-208.

Clarke (1916-1938)

Clarke (A.W.H.), Editor, Miscellanea Genealogica et Heraldica. The years cited are those on the title pages of the bound volumes edited by him. Earlier volumes were edited by Howard (q.v.) and by Bannerman (q.v.). The "1916" volume, edited by both Bannerman and Clarke, is cited under Bannerman; the first volume edited by Clarke alone was "1916-1917". Two items by Sir T. Innes of Learney are cited under his name.

College of Arms Bill (1973)

The College of Arms Bill, in The Genealogists' Magazine XVII (1972-1974), No.7 (September 1973), 355-364.

Collins (1946)

Collins (S.M.), Differencing in English Medieval Heraldry, in The Antiquaries' Journal XXVI (1946), 172-174.

Courthope (1863)

Courthope (W.), Return from the College of Arms, in The Herald and Genealogist I (1863), 464-469.

Dallaway (1793)

Dallaway (J.), Inquiries into the Origin and Progress of the Science of Heraldry in England (1793).

Dennys (1982)

Dennys (R.O.), Heraldry and the Heralds (1982).

Dickson (1877)

Dickson (T.), Preface to Accounts of the Lord High Treasurer of Scotland, Volume I (1877).

Doubleday (1916)

Doubleday (H.A.), Earldoms and Baronies in History and in Law, and the Doctrine of Abeyance, in The Complete Peerage, New Edition IV (1916), 651-753. See also Notes by G.E.C. on pages 754-760.

Dugdale (1811)

Dugdale (Sir W.), The Antient Usage in bearing of such Ensigns of Honour as are commonly called Arms (reprinted with other works edited by T.C.Banks, 1811).

Edmondson (1780)

Edmondson (J.), A Complete Body of Heraldry (1780).

Flynn (1978)

Flynn (J.E.), Recent Matriculations of Interest, in The Double Tressure (3 August 1978), 7-12.

FMN (1865)

F.M.N., The Law of Inheritance as applied to Arms, in The Herald and Genealogist II (1865), 1-22

Forrester (1983)

Forrester (C.D.I.G.), The Heraldry and Insignia of the Baronage of Scotland, in The Coat of Arms, New Series V (No.126) (1983), 157-166.

Fox-Davies (1949)

Fox-Davies (A.C.), A Complete Guide to Heraldry (1949).

Full Report (1955)

The Full Report of the Case of the Mayor ... of Manchester ... in the High Court of Chivalry published by The Heraldry Society (1955).

Gayre (1958)

Gayre of Gayre and Nigg (G.R.), Letter in The Coat of Arms V (No.35) (1958), 81-83.

Gayre (1961)

Gayre of Gayre and Nigg (G.R.), Heraldic Cadency (1961).

Gayre and Gayre (1964-1969)

Gayre of Gayre and Nigg (G.R.) and Gayre of Gayre and Nigg, Younger (R.), Roll of Scottish Arms, Part I (1964-1969).

Gibbs (1913)

Gibbs (V.), Surrender of Peerages in England, in The Complete Peerage, New Edition III (1913), 589-591.

Grant (1945)

Grant (Sir F.J.), Court of the Lord Lyon 1318-1945 (1945),

Grazebrook (1890)

Grazebrook (G.), The Dates of variously-shaped Shields, with coincident Dates and Examples (1890).

Guillim (1666)

Guillim (J.), et: al., A Display of Heraldrie ("Sixth" Edition, 1666) (a different "sixth edition" appeared in 1724).

Harmon (1977)

Harmon (J.F.), The Heraldry of the illegitimate Children of Louis XV, in The Coat of Arms, New Series II (No.101)(1977), 118-121.

Harwood (1895-1922)

Harwood (H.W.F.), Editor, The Genealogist, New Series XI-XXXVIII. The years cited are those on the title pages of the bound volumes. Earlier volumes cited were edited by Marshall (q.v.).

Heraldica (1940)

"Heraldica", The Arms of Duffus of Claverhouse, in Notes and Queries CLXXVIII (1940), 74, 78, 93-96, 131-133.

Heraldica (1942)

"Heraldica", Heraldry and "War-leadership", in Notes and Queries CLXXXIII (1942), 92-100.

Hope and Wagner (1953)

Hope (Sir W.H. St.J.), A Grammar of English Heraldry, revised by Sir A.R.Wagner (1953).

Howard (1866-1902)

Howard (J.J.), Editor, Miscellanea Genealogica et Heraldica. The years cited are those on the title pages of the bound volumes of the various series edited by him. Later volumes were edited by Bannerman (q.v.) and by Clarke (q.v.).

Howard and Chester (1880-1883)

Howard (J.J.) and Chester (J.L.), The Visitation of London Anno Domini 1633, 1634 and 1635 (Harleian Society Publications XV and XVII) (Volume I: 1880; Volume II (edited by Howard alone): 1883).

Innes (1929)

Innes of Learney (Sir T.), Heraldry, in Encyclopaedia of the Laws of Scotland VII (1929).

Innes (1930)

Innes of Learney (Sir T.), Lyon King-of-Arms, in Encyclopaedia of the Laws of Scotland IX (1930).

Innes (1933)

Innes of Learney (Sir T.), Transfers of Armorial Bearings, in Scottish Notes and Queries XI (Third Series) (1933), 187-189.

Innes (1938A)

Innes of Learney (Sir T.), Chisholm of Chisholm Matriculation, in Miscellanea Genealogica et Heraldica, Fifth Series X (1938), 97.

Innes (1938B)

Innes of Learney (Sir T.), Farquharson of Invercauld Matriculation, in Miscellanea Genealogica et Heraldica, Fifth Series X (1938), 121.

Innes (1940A)

Innes of Learney (Sir T.), Armorial Tailzies in Scotland, in Notes and Queries CLXXVIII (1940), 254-257, 272-275, 293-297.

Innes (1940B)

Innes of Learney (Sir T.), The Ensigns-armorial of Erskine of Linlathen, in Notes and Queries CLXXIX (1940), 308-311.

Innes (1940C)

Innes of Learney (Sir T.), Heraldic "Legitimation", in Notes and Queries CLXXIX (1940), 362-365.

Innes (1940D)

Innes of Learney (Sir T.), The Nature of Armorial Bearings, in Notes and Queries CLXXVIII (1940),362-367.

Innes (1940E)

Innes of Learney (Sir T.), Diploma of Nobility for de Landa, in The Juridical Review (1940), 181-221

Innes (1941A)

Innes of Learney (Sir T.), Armorial Conveyancing, in Notes and Queries CLXXX (1941), 128-133.

Innes (1941B)

Innes of Learney (Sir T.), Sir George Mackenzie on Armorial Succession, in Notes and Queries CLXXXI (1941), 2-4.

Innes (1946)

Innes of Learney (Sir T.), The Robes of the Feudal Baronage of Scotland, in Proceedings of the Society of Antiquaries of Scotland LXXIX (1946), 111-163

Innes and Innes (1978)

Innes of Learney (Sir T.), Scots Heraldry, revised by M.R.lnnes of Edingight (1978).

Lart (1938)

Lart (C.E.), Pedigrees and Papers of James Terry, Athlone Herald (1939).

Littledale (1925-1926)

Littledale (W.A.), A Collection of Miscellaneous Grants (Harleian Society Publications LXXVI, LXXVII) (1925-1926).

London (1952)

London (H.S.), A Catalogue of the English Officers of Arms, in Burke's Landed Gentry, Seventeenth Edition (1952), cvii-cxxi. See also Wagner and London (1963).

London (1970)

London (H.S.), The Life of William Bruges, the first Garter King of Arms (Harleian Society Publications CXI, CXII) (1970).

London and Wagner (1949)

London (H.S.) and Wagner (Sir A.R.), Heralds of the Nobility, in The Complete Peerage, New Edition XI (1949), 39-104.

McFarlane (1973)

McFarlane (K.B.,), The Nobility of later Medieval England (1973).

Mackenzie (1680)

Mackenzie of Rosehaugh (Sir G.), The Science of Heraldry, treated as a Part of the Civil Law (1680).

Markland (1865)

Markland (J.H.), The Proofs of Arms required by the Heralds at their Visitations, in The Herald and Genealogist II (1865), 149-154.

Marshall (1877-1883)

Marshall (G.W.), Editor, The Genealogist, I-VII. The years cited are those on the titlepages of the bound volumes. Later volumes cited are among those edited by Harwood (q.v.).

Monncreiffe (1982)

Monncreiffe of that Ilk (Sir I.), Some Comments on "New Clans and Grants of Arms", in The Coat of Arms, New Series V (No.121) (1982), 8-17.

Nichols (1863-1874)

Nichols (J.G.), Editor, The Herald and Genealogist, I-VIII. The years cited are those on the titlepages of the bound volumes. Some specific items by other persons are cited under their names.

Nisbet (1722-1742)

Nisbet (A.), A System of Heraldry (first part, 1722; second part, 1742).

Norton (1982)

Norton (R.), The Arms of Eustace Hatch and Others, in The Coat of Arms, New Series V (No.121) (1982), 18-19.

Observations (1724)

Observations on the Office and Officers of Arms ..., in Guillim (J.), et al., A Display of Heraldry, The Sixth Edition (Section entitled The Second Part of Honour Civil and a Collection of Tracts ...) (1724), 42-58.

P (1955)

The Law Reports: Probate, Divorce and Admiralty Division (1955).

Paul (1903)

Paul (Sir J.B.), An Ordinary of Arms contained in the Public Register of all Arms and Bearings in Scotland (Second Edition, 1903). Continued by Reid and Wilson (q.v.).

Phillimore (1903A)

Phillimore (W.P.W.), Heralds' College and Coats of Arms regarded from a legal aspect (Second Edition, 1903).

Phillimore (1903B)

Phillimore (W.P.W.), Prescriptive Usage of Arms, in The Ancestor V (April 1903), 222-223. See also The Ancestor VII (October 1903), 267-268.

Pine (1963)

Pine (L.G.), The Story of Heraldry (1963).

Reid and Wilson (1977)

Reid of Robertland (D.) and Wilson (D.N.), An Ordinary of Arms, Volume II (1977).

Round (1907)

Round (J.H.), Studies in Peerage and Family History (1907).

Round (1910)

Round (J.H.), Peerage and Pedigree (1910).

Ruvigny (1904)

Ruvigny and Raineval (M.H.Massue, Marquis de), The Jacobite Peerage (1904).

Rylands (1902)

Rylands (J.P.), An early Grant of Arms, in The Genealogist, New Series XVIII (1902), 35.

Rylands (1911)

Rylands (W.H.), The Visitation of the County of Warwick ... in 1682 ... and ... 1683 (Harleian Society Publications LXII) (1911).

Rylands and Bannerman (1922)

Rylands (W.H.) and Bannerman (W.B.), The Visitation of the County of Rutland ... in 1681 ... and ... 1682 (Harleian Society Publications LXXIII) (1922).

Saltire Argent (1979)

"Saltire Argent", Letter in The Double Tressure (4 March 1979), 10-11.

Schomberg (1908)

Schomberg (A.), Grant of Arms to Morgan, in The Genealogist, New Series XXIV (1908), 138-139.

Scott-Giles (1960)

Scott-Giles (C.W.), Augmentations for Loyalty, in The Coat of Arms VI (No.42) (1960), 51-56.

Seton (1863)

Seton (G.), The Law and Practice of Heraldry in Scotland (1863).

Sitwell (1902)

Sitwell (Sir G.R.), The English Gentleman, in The Ancestor I (April 1902), 58-103.

Squibb (1956)

Squibb (G.D.), Reports of Heraldic Cases in the Court of Chivalry (Harleian Society Publications CVII) (1956).

Squibb (1959)

Squibb (G.D.), The High Court of Chivalry (1959).

Squibb (1967)

Squibb (G.D.), The Law of Arms in England (Second Edition, 1967).

Squibb (1967H)

Squibb (G.D.), Heralds and Pursuivants Extraordinary, in The Coat of Arms IX (No.71)(1967), 238-243; (No.72) (1967), 274-282.

Squibb (1978)

Squibb (G.D.), Visitation Pedigrees and the Genealogist (1978).

Squibb (1981)

Squibb (G.D.), Peerages and Dignities, in Halsbury's Laws of England (Fourth Edition) XXXV (1981), 441-479.

Squibb (1985)

Squibb (G.D.), Munimenta Heraldica (Harleian Society Publications, New Series 4)(1985), (A collection of documents relevant to some aspects of the English laws of arms, including royal Letters Patent, Warrants, Declarations and Commissions; Orders of the Earl Marshal; etc.).

Stevenson (1914)

Stevenson (J.H.), Heraldry in Scotland (1914).

Stevenson (1926)

Stevenson (J.H.), Memorandum on the Office and Court of the Lyon King of Arms (1926).

Stewart (1974)

Stewart of Ardvorlich (J.), The Camerons: A History Clan Cameron (1974).

Wagner (1956)

Wagner (Sir A.R.), Heralds and Heraldry in the Middle Ages (Second Edition, 1956).

Wagner (1967)

Wagner (Sir A.R.), Heralds of England, a History of the Office and College of Arms (1967).

Wagner (1978)

Wagner (Sir A.R.), Heralds and Ancestors (1978).

Wagner and London (1963)

The College of Arms ... by W.H. Godfrey ... assisted by Sir A. Wagner ... with a complete list of the Officers of Arms prepared by ... H. S. London (1963).

Walker (1963)

Walker (D.M.), The Scottish Legal System (Second Edition, 1963).

Watson (1898)

Watson (G.W.), Two Earls of Winchester, in The Genealogist, New Series XIV (1898), 73-79.

Woodward and Burnett (1892)

Woodward (J.) and Burnett (G.), A Treatise on Heraldry British and Foreign (1892, facsimile re-print 1969).

X (1900)

"X", The Right to bear Arms (1900).

FRENCH LANGUAGE

Adam (1957)

Adam (P.), Les Armoiries bourgeoises et la Thèse de M. Chabanne, in Archivum heraldicum (1957), 9-10.

Adam-Even (1949)

Adam-Even (P.), Un Armorial français du milieu du XIIIe, in Archives héraldiques suisses (1949), 15-22, 68-75, 115-121.

Adam-Even (1957)

Adam-Even (P.), Les Fonctions militaires des Hérauts d'armes, in Archives héraldiques suisses (1957), 2-33.

Adam-Even (1961-1968)

Adam-Even (P.), L'Armorial universel du Héraut Gelre, in Archives héraldiques suisses (1961), 48-57; (1962), 68-73; (1963), 63-79; (1964), 75-80; (1965), 70-82; (1967), 72-83; (1968), 70-83.

Anselme (1726-1733)

Père Anselme, Histoire généalogique et chronologique de la Maison Royale de France … continuée per M. du Fourny (Third Edition, 1726-1733).

Armorial Général (1696-1709)

Armorial Général, containing the arms registered in pursuance of the Edict of 1696. The manuscript volumes are in the Bibliothèque Nationale in Paris.

Arundel de Condé (1981)

Arundel de Condé (G.), Anoblissements, Maintenues et Réhabilitations en Normandie 1598-1790 (1981).

Bacquet (1744)

Les Œuvres de M. Jean Bacquet. Augmentées … par M. Claude-Joseph de Ferrière (1744).

Bara (1628)

Bara (J.de), Le Blason des Armoiries … reveu, corrigé et augmenté … par B.R.D.E.L.R. (1628)

Barbier (1856)

Barbier (E.J.F.), Journal historique et anecdotique du Règne de Louis XV (1847-1856); we cite only Volume IV (1856).

Belleguise (1923)

Belleguise (A.), Les Maintenues de Noblesse en Provence, edited by A. du Roure (1923).

Belleval (1867)

Belleval (R.de), Toison-d'Or et sa Famille, in Revue nobiliaire, historique et biographique, Nouvelle Série III (1867), 529-540.

Blanc (1975)

Blanc (F.P.), Concession d'Armoiries timbrées et Anoblissement d'apres la Jurisprudence provençale moderne, in Provence historique XXV (1975), 525-550.

Bluche and Durye (1962)

Bluche (F.), and Durye (P.), L'Anoblissement par Charge avant 1789 (1962).

Boisseau (1657)

Boisseau (J.), Promptuaire armorial (1657). (References herein are to the First Part.)

Borel d'Hauterive (1843-1891)

Borel d'Hauterive (A.F.J.), Annuaire de la Noblesse de France (1843-1891).

Bosredon (1892)

Bosredon (P.de), Notes pour servir la Sigilographie du Departement de la Haute-Vienne (1892).

Bouchot (1875)

Bouchot (H.), Armorial Général de France, Généralité de Bourgogne (Franche-Comté) (1875).

Boulaud (1910)

Boulaud (J.), Les Armoiries de Jean Vidaud du Dognon, in Bulletin de la Société Archéologique et Historique du Limousin LX (1910), 191-257.

Bouton (1863-1877)

Bouton (V.), Le Héraut d'armes (1863-1877).

Bouvot (1628)

Bouvot (J.), Nouveau Recueil des Arrêts de Bourgogne Volume II (1628).

Brillon (1711)

Brillon (P.J.), Dictionnaire des Arrests, ou Jurisprudence universelle des Parlemens de France ... (1711).

Brisson and Charondas Le Caron (1609)

Brisson (P.), Le Code du Roy Henry III ... augmenté ... par L. Charondas Le Caron (1609).

Cadot (1697)

C ... (i.e. T. Cadot), Le Blason de France, ou Notes curieuses sur l'Edit concernant la Police des Armoiries (1697).

Chambois and Farcy (1895)

Chambois (E.L.) and Farcy (P.de), Recherche de la Noblesse dans la Généralité de Tours en 1666 (1895).

Chamillart (1887-1889)

Chamillart (G.), Généralité de Caen, Recherche de la Noblesse faite par Ordre du Roi en 1666 et années suivantes, edited by A. du Buisson de Courson (1887-1889).

Chassin du Guerny (1930)

Chassin du Guerny (R.), Charles D'Hozier - Armorial Général de France - Bretagne (1930).

Chaussinand-Nogaret (1976)

Chaussinand-Nogaret (G.), La Noblesse au XVIIIe siècle, De la Féodalite aux Lumières (1976).

Cherin (1788)

Cherin (L.N.H.), Abrégé chronologique d'Edits, Declarations, Réglemens, Arrêts et Lettres-patentes des Rois de France ... concernant le fait de Noblesse (1788). This work is partly based on D'Hozier (1738-1768) Register I, Second Part. It was republished in P. J. Migne, Nouvelle Encyclopédie théologique XIII (1861). A facsimile edition of the original was published in 1974.

Contamine (1976)

Contamine (P.), Introduction, in La noblesse au moyen age, Essais à la mémoire de Robert Boutruche (1976).

Cumont (1890)

Cumont (M.T.P.de), Recherches sur la Noblesse du Périgord (1890).

Des Diguères (1865)

Des Diguères (V.G.), Sevigni, on une Paroisse rurale en Normandie (1865).

Dessalles (1847-1848)

Dessalles (A.), Histoire générale des Antilles (1847-1848).

Dessalles and Frémont (1974)

Dessalles (A.) and Frémont (H.de), Histoire et Généalogie de la Famille Dessalles ou des Salles (1974).

D'Haucourt and Durivault (1965)

D'Haucourt (G.) and Durivault (G.), Le Blason (1965).

D'Hozier (1738-1768)

D'Hozier (L.P.) and D'Hozier de Serigny (A.M.), Armorial Général de la France, ou Registres de la Noblesse de France (1738-1768). Register I, Second Part, contains summaries of various statutes on nobility; most of this material is in Cherin (1788), and the notes herein refer only to the latter, except where D'Hozier gives a relevant detail not in Cherin.

Du Boscq de Beaumont (1906)

Du Boscq de Beaumont (G.), La Jurisprudence héraldique des d'Hozier, in Annuaire du Conseil heraldique de France XIX (1906), 165-177.

Dufau de Maluquer (1889)

Dufau de Maluquer (A.) and Jaurgain (J.B.E.de), Armorial de Béarn 1696-1701 (part published)(1889).

Du Lis (1856)

Du Lis (C.), Opuscules historiques relatifs à Jeanne Darc (1856).

Du Puy de Clinchamps (1978)

Du Puy de Clinchamps (P.), La Noblesse, revised by P. du Puy de Clinchamps (1978).

Dupuy Demportes (1754)

Dupuy Demportes (J.B.), Traité historique et moral du Blason (1754)

Durand de Saint-Front (1968)

Durand de Saint-Front (J.), La Recherche de la Noblesse de l'Election de Valognes de 1523, in Revue du Departement de la Manche X (1968), 187-216, 239-289.

Du Roure de Paulin (1906)

Du Roure de Paulin (E.du F.), Les Rois, Hérauts et Poursuivants d'Armes (1906).

Durye (1974)

Durye (P.), Introduction to the 1974 facsimile reprint of Cherin (1788).

Expilly (1636)

Plaidoyez de Messire Claude Expilly, Chevalier, Conseiller du Roy en son Conseil d'Etat … cinquième Edition, reveue et augmentée (1636).

Fauchet (1606)

Fauchet (C.), Origines des Chevaliers, Armoiries et Heraux (Second Edition, 1606).

Favyn (1620)

Favyn (A.), Le Théatre d'Honneur et de Chevalerie (1620).

Ferrières and Boucher d'Argis (1787)

Ferrières (C.J.de) and Boucher d'Argis (A.G.), Dictionnaire de droit et de pratique, Nouvelle édition (1787).

Figon (1580)

Figon (C.de), Discours des Estats et Offices (1580).

Galbreath and Jéquier (1977)

Galbreath (D.L.) and Jéquier (L.), Manuel du Blason (1977).

Geliot (1635)

Geliot (L.), Indice armorial (1635).

Geliot and Palliot (1661)

Geliot (L.), La Vraye et parfaite Science des Armoiries, ou Indice armorial, augmenté par Pierre Palliot (1661).

Gentil de Rosmorduc (1891)

Gentil de Rosmorduc (A.N.), Preuves de Noblesse des Demoiselles bretonnes admises à Saint-Cyr (1891).

Cosset (1903)

Cosset (P.), Armorial de l'Election de Reims, dressé par C. d'Hozier (1903).

Grandmaison (1904-1905)

Grandmaison (L.de), Essai d'Armorial des Artistes Français (XVI-XVIIIe siècle) (1904-1905).

Grolée-Virville (1978)

Grolée-Virville (A.de), Les d'Hozier, Juges d'Armes de France (1978).

Hallez d'Arros (1891)

Hallez d'Arros (C.H.O.), L'Armorial Général de France (1891).

Jougla (1934-1952)

Jougla de Morenas (H.), Grand Armorial de France, Catalogue général des Armoiries des Familles nobles de France. Volumes I-IV, published respectively in 1934, 1938, 1935 (sic) and 1939, were edited by Jougla himself; Volumes V and VI, published in 1948 and 1949, by R. de Warren; and Supplement, published in 1952, by A. Frantzen.

La Bigne de Villeneuve (1918)

La Bigne de Villeneuve (M.), La Dérogeance de la Noblesse (1918, reprinted 1977).

La Bouralière (1892-1893)

La Bouralière (A.de), Maintenues de Noblesse prononcées par ... Intendants de la Généralité de Poitiers, in Archives Historiques du Poitou XXII-XXIII (1892-1893).

La Force (1972)

La Force (Duc de), Les brisures des Montmorency, in Genealogica et Heraldica (10th International Congress of Genealogical and Heraldic Sciences, Vienna 1970) (1972).

La Roche-Flavin and Graverol (1745)

Arrests notables du Parlement de Toulouse. Nouvelle Edition (1745).

La Roque (1734)

La Roque (G.A.de), Traité de la Noblesse … Nouvelle Edition augmentée des Traités du Blason des Armoiries de France, de l'Origine des Noms Sur-Noms, et du Ban et Arrière-Ban (1734).

La Roque and Barthélemy (1864)

La Roque (L.de) and Barthélemy (E.M.de), Catalogue des Certificats de Noblesse délivrés par Cherin pour le Service militaire 1781-1789 (1864).

La Roque and Barthélemy (1865)

La Roque (L.de) and Barthélemy (E.M.de), Catalogue de la Noblesse des Colonies (1865).

La Villegille (1856)

La Villegille (A.de), Notes in Barbier (1856).

Leber (1838)

Leber (C.), Collection des Meilleurs Dissertations, Notices et Traités particuliers relatifs à l'Histoire de France, Volume XIII (1838).

Le Feron (1555)

Le Feron (J.), De la primitive Institution des Roys, Herauldz, et Poursuivans d'Armes (1555).

Le Feron and Godefroy (1658)

Le Feron (J.) and Godefroy (D.), Histoire des Connestables, Chanceliers, et Gardes des Seaux, Mareschaux, Admiraux … (1658).

Lefevre de Caumartin (1673)

Lefevre de Caumartin (L.F.), Procès verbal de la Noblesse de Champagne (1673).

Le Second Ordre (1973)

Le Second Ordre (1947, reprinted 1973).

Magneney (1633)

Magneney (C.), Le Recueil des Armes de plusieurs nobles Maisons et Families. The copy examined, which is in the British Library, contains a statement that the printing was finished on 30 July 1633, but some of the pages are perhaps of a later date.

Marion (1923)

Marion (M.), Dictionnaire des Institutions de la France aux XVIIe et XVIIIe siècles (1923).

Martres (1847)

Martres (A.de), Revue historique de la Noblesse III (1847).

Mathieu (1946)

Mathieu (R.M.), Le Système héraldique français (1946).

Maugard (1788)

Maugard (A.), Remarques sur la Noblesse (Second Edition, 1788).

Melleville (1867)

Melleville (-), Enquête de 1666 sur la Noblesse de la Généralité de Soissons (Election de Laon), in Revue nobiliaire historique et biographique, Nouvelle Série III (1867), 218-228, 264-278.

Menestrier (1661)

Menestrier (C.F.), L'Art du Blason justifié (1661).

Menestrier (1665)

Menestrier (C.F.), Abrégé méthodique des Principes Héraldiques (1665).

Menestrier (1696)

Menestrier (C.F.), La nouvelle Méthode raisonnée du Blason (1696).

Menestrier and Lemoine (1780)

Menestrier (C.F.), La nouvelle Méthode raisonnée ... mise dans un meilleur ordre et augmentée (by P.C. Lemoine) (1780).

Meurgey de Tupigny (1965-1967)

Meurgey de Tupigny (J.), Armorial de la Généralité de Paris dressé par Charles d'Hozier en execution de l'Edit de novembre 1696 (1965-1967).

Meyer (1966)

Meyer (J.), La Noblesse bretonne au XVIIIe siècle (1966).

Meyer (1972)

Meyer (J.), La Noblesse bretonne au XVIIIe siecle (1972). This is a condensed version of Meyer (1966), with the complete omission of some sections.

Montgrand (1864)

Montgrand (G.de), Armorial de la Ville de Marseille (1864).

Moreau (1630)

Moreau (P.), Le Tableau des Armoiries de France (1630)

Moreau de Pravieux (1894)

Moreau de Pravieux (J.), Armorial Général de France, Generalite de Limoges (1894).

Olivier and Vialet (1927)

Olivier (E.) and Vialet (G.), Essai de Répertoire des Ex-libris et Fers de Reliure des Médecins et des Pharmaciens français (1927).

Pastoret (1811-1840)

Pastoret (C.E.J.P.de), Ordonnances des Rois de France de la troisième Race XV-XX (1811-1840).

Pinoteau (1976)

Pinoteau (H.), Introduction to the 1976 facsimile reprint of Menestrier's La Méthode du Blason (1688).

Prevost (1910)

Prevost (G.A.), Armorial Général de France, Généralité de Rouen (1910).

Prevost (1913)

Prevost (G.A.), Armorial Général de France, Généralité de Caen (1913).

Prevost (1922-1924)

Prevost (G.A.), Armorial Général de France, Généralité d'Alençon (1922-1924).

Prinet (1909)

Prinet (M.), Les Armoiries écartelées des Conjoints d'après les Sceaux français, in Revue numismatique (1909), 372-382.

Prinet (1917)

Prinet (M.), L'Ordonnance de Henri II, donnée à Amboise … , in Bulletin de la Société nationale des Antiquaires de France (1917), 147-154.

Prinet (1932)

Prinet (M.), Les Armoiries des Français dans le Poème du Siège de Carlaverock (1932).

Quicherat (1841-1845)

Quicherat (J.E.J.), Procès de Condamnation et de Réhabilitation de Jeanne d'Arc (1841-1845).

Rabino (1940)

Rabino (H.L.), Ex-libris d'Arthur Villettes, in Archives héraldiques suisses (1940).

Ribier (1907-1912)

Ribier (L.de), Preuves de la Noblesse d'Auvergne (1907-1912).

Rivoire de La Batie (1867)

Rivoire de La Batie (G.de), Armorial de Dauphiné (1867).

Sailly (1870)

Sailly (C.de), Les Fleurs de Lis en Champ d'Azur, in Revue historique, nobiliaire et biographique, Nouvelle Série VI (1870-1871), 174-176.

Sauvage (1925)

Sauvage (R.N.), Documents sur Guillaume Houel, in Mélanges de la Société de l'Histoire de Normandie, Ninth Series (1925), 281-321.

Scohier (1597)

Scohier (J.), L'Estat et Comportement des Armes (1597).

Segoing (1657)

Segoing (C.), Trésor héraldique ou Mercure armorial (1657).

Segoing (1660)

Segoing (C.), Armorial universal (1660).

Sereville and Saint Simon (1975-1977)

Sereville (E.de) and Saint Simon (F.de), Dictionnaire de la Noblesse française (1975), and Supplement (1977).

Signac (1559)

Le Trespas, et Ordre des Obsèques ... de feu ... le Roy Henri deuxième de ce nom ... par le Seigneur de la Borde, François de Signac, Roy d'Armes de Dauphiné (1559).

Terrebasse (1850)

Terrebasse (P.L.E.A.J.de), Relation des principaux Evenements de la Vie de Salvaing de Boissieu (1850).

Tesson (1897)

Tesson (A.de), Armorial des Elections d'Avranches et de Mortain, in Mémoires de la Société d'Archéologie, Littérature, Sciences et Arts des Arrondissements d'Avranches et de Mortain XIII (1897), 1-184.

Tesson (1899)

Tesson (A.de), La Recherche de Jean Guilloches, Elu de Mortain, en 1523, in Mémoires de la Société d'Archéologie, Littérature, Sciences et Arts des Arrondissements d'Avranches et de Mortain XIV (1899), 1-132.

Thounens (1789)

Thounens (J.E.), Almanach historique, chronologique ... pour les Colonies, Année 1790 (1789).

Toulgouet-Treanna (1901)

Toulgouet-Treanna (E.de), Les Recherches de Noblesse en Berry, in Mémoires de la Société des Antiquaires du Centre XXIV 1900 (1901), 87-360.

Vallet de Viriville (1866)

Vallet de Viriville (A.), Introduction to Armorial de France, Angleterre, Ecosse, ... par Gilles Le Bouvier, dit Berry, ... publié par M. Vallet (de Viriville) (1866).

Varennes (1640)

Varennes (M.G.de), Le Roy d'Armes, ou l'Art de bien former ... toutes les sortes d'Armoiries (Second Edition, 1640).

Vulson de La Colombière (1838)

Vulson de La Colombière (M.), De l'Office des Roys d'Armes, des Heraults et des Poursuivans. This work, first published in 1645, is cited as reprinted in Leber (1838).